Math ADVANTAGE

W9-AUF-246

Performance Assessment

TEACHER'S GUIDE

- INTERVIEW/TASK TESTS
- QUARTERLY EXTENDED PERFORMANCE ASSESSMENTS
  SCORING RUBRICS
  SAMPLE STUDENT PAPERS
  PERFORMANCE INDICATORS
  ANSWER KEYS
- MANAGEMENT FORMS

Grade 5

Harcourt Brace & Company

rlando • Atlanta • Austin • Boston • San Francisco • Chicago • Dallas • New York • Toronto • London

http://www.hbschool.com

ISBN 0-15-311182-8

7 8 9 10 11 12 13 14 15 16   022 2006 2005 2004 2003 2002 2001

CONTENTS

▶ Evalulating Interview/Task Test Items

▶ Interview Task/Test and Evaluation Criteria

Performance Assessment Program

Unique Features of Math Advantage Performance Assessment

To create assessments that actually evaluate what is taught, it is necessary to target specific math concepts, skills, and strategies at each grade level. In planning the assessment program for *Math Advantage,* a review was made of performance assessments cited in professional literature and also of those used in state testing programs. Comparisons were made among available models and desirable features were identified. Holistic scoring was chosen as the primary method of scoring. The *Math Advantage* Performance assessments offer the following features:

- **They model good instruction**
  The assessments are like mini lessons.

- **They are diagnostic.**
  By reviewing students' notes, teachers gain valuable insight into the thinking strategies that students are using.

- **They encourage the thinking process.**
  The assessments guide students through the process of organizing their thoughts and revising their strategies as they solve problems.

- **They are flexible.**
  No strict time limits are imposed,and students are encourage to proceed at their own pace.

- **They use authentic instruction.**
  Each task is based on realistic problem-solving situations.

- **They are scored holistically.**
  Each student's responses are scored holistically to provide a comprehensive view of his or her performance.

Development of the Performance Assessment Program

Each assessment was field-tested with students before it was selected for inclusion in the program. After the assessments were selected, the pool of student papers for each assessment was reviewed and model papers were selected to illustrate the various scores. Annotations were then written for each model paper, explaining why the score was given.

The development process provided an opportunity to drop or correct those assessments that were not working as expected.

Administering the Performance Assessments

- **Be encouraging.**
  Your role in administering the assessments should be that of a coach, motivating, guiding, and encouraging students to produce their best work.

- **Be clear.**
  The directions for the assessments are not standardized. If necessary, you may rephrase them for students.

- **Be supportive.**
  You may assist students who need help. The amount of assistance needed will vary depending on the needs and abilities of your students.

- **Be fair.**
  Allow students adequate time to do their best work. They should not feel that they could have done better if they had been given enough time.

- **Be flexible.**
  All students need not proceed through the assessments at the same rate and in the same manner.

- **Be involving.**
  Whenever possible, involve students in the evaluation process.

Providing for Students with Special Needs

Many school districts are facing the challenge of adapting instruction and assessment to make them appropriate for their learners with special needs. Because the performance assessments are not standardized, the procedure for administering them can be adjusted to meet the needs of these learners. Teachers can help students who have difficulty responding by

- pairing a less proficient learner with a more proficient learner.

- encouraging students to discuss their ideas with a partner.

- providing an audiotape of the performance assessment and having students read along with the narration.

- permitting students to record tapes their response in lieu of a writing them.

- allowing students to do their initial planning, computing, designing, and drafting on the computer.

- giving students extra time to do their planning.

- providing assistance upon request.

Keep in mind, however, that the more the performance assessments are modified, the less reliable they may be as measures of students' mathematical ability.

Scoring Rubrics for Mathematics

In scoring a student's task, the teacher should ask two questions: *How well did the student use the conventions of mathematics to arrive at a solution?* and *How well did the student communicate the solution* The scoring system used for the performance assessments is designed to be compatible with those used by many state assessment programs. Using a 4-point scale, the teacher classifies the student's performance as "excellent," "adequate," "limited," or "little or no achievement". A Score 3 paper shows evidence of extensive understanding of content and provides an exceptionally clear and effective solution. A Score 2 paper shows an acceptable understanding of content and provides a solution that shows reasonable insight. A Score 1 paper shows partial understanding and is clear in some parts, but not in others. A Score 0 paper demonstrates poor understanding of content and provides a solution that is unclear.

4-Point Scale			
Excellent Achievement	Adequate Achievement	Limited Achievement	Little or No Achievement
3	2	1	0

Sharing Results with Students and Parents

The performance assessment can provide valuable insights into students' mathematical abilities by revealing how all students performed on a common task. However, it is important that their performance on the assessment be interpreted in light of other samples that have been collected such as daily papers, student portfolios, and other types of tests, as well as teacher observation.

For Students

Discuss the rubric with students and explain how it is used. You may even want to score some anonymous papers as a group or have students score each other's papers and discuss the criteria as they apply to those papers. Make photocopies of the rubrics to use for individual reports. Discuss the reports in conferences with students, pointing out their strengths as well as areas in which they could still improve.

For Parents

Results of performance assessments may also be shared with parents, who will. appreciate seeing what their children can do. Show parents the performance assessment so that they understand the task that the students were asked to perform. Show their child's responses and discuss the strengths and weaknesses of the responses. Explain the scoring rubric and how the responses were evaluated. Show parents model papers that illustrate the range in student performance to help them put their child's paper in perspective.

Using Results to Assign Grades

No single test, whether a standardized achievement test, a performance assessment, or an open-ended test, can fully measure a student's mathematical ability. For this reason it is important to use multiple measures of assessment. Therefore, a score on performance assessment should not be used as the sole determiner of a report-card grade or semester grade. The performance assessment could represent one of several factors used to determine a student's grade. Assessments could be combined with the results of a selection of tests, daily grades, class participation, self-reflections, and various samples collected in a portfolio. The following table shows how holistic scores can be converted into numerical or letter grades.

Holistic Score	Letter Grade	Numerical Grade
3	A	90-100
2	B	80-89
1	C	70-79
0	D-F	60 or below

Developing Your Own Rubric

A well-written rubric can help teachers score students' work more accurately and fairly. It also gives students a better idea of what qualities their work should exhibit. Using performance assessment to make connections between teaching and learning requires both conceptual and reflective involvement. Determining criteria may be the most difficult aspect of the process of developing assessment criteria on which to evaluate students' performance. Particularly challenging is the task of finding the right language to describe the qualities of student performance that distinguishes mediocre and excellent work. Teachers should begin the process of developing rubrics by

- gathering sample rubrics as models to be adapted as needed.

- selecting samples of students' work that represent a range of quality.

- determining the qualities of work that distinguish good examples from poor examples.

- using those qualities to write descriptors for the desired characteristics.

- continually revising the criteria until the rubric score reflects the quality of work indicated.

Your Own **Scoring Rubric**

Response Level	Criteria
Score 3	**Generally accurate, complete, and clear** _____ _____ _____ _____
Score 2	**Partially accurate, complete, and clear** _____ _____ _____ _____
Score 1	**Minimally accurate, complete, and clear** _____ _____ _____ _____
Score 0	**Not accurate, complete, and clear** _____ _____ _____ _____

Math Advantage **Scoring Rubric**

Response Level	Criteria
Score 3	**Generally accurate, complete, and clear** _____ All or most parts of the task are successfully completed; the intents of all parts of the task are addressed with appropriate strategies and procedures. _____ There is evidence that the student has a clear understanding of key concepts and procedures. _____ Student work and explanations are clear. _____ Additional illustrations or information, if present, enhance communication. _____ Answers for all parts are correct or reasonable.
Score 2	**Partially accurate, complete, and clear** _____ Some parts of the task are successfully completed; other parts are attempted and their intents addressed, but they are not successfully completed. _____ There is evidence that the student has partial understanding of key concepts and procedures. _____ Some student work and explanations are clear, but it is necessary to make inferences to understand the response. _____ Additional illustrations or information, if present, may not enhance communication significantly. _____ Answers for some parts are correct, but partially correct or incorrect for others.
Score 1	**Minimally accurate, complete, and clear** _____ A part (or parts) of the task is (are) addressed with minimal success while other parts are omitted or incorrect. _____ There is minimal or limited evidence that the student understands concepts and procedures. _____ Student work and explanations may be difficult to follow, and it is necessary to fill in the gaps to understand the response. _____ Additional illustrations or information, if present, do not enhance communication and may be irrelevant. _____ Answers to most parts are incorrect.
Score 0	**Not accurate, complete, and clear** _____ No part of the task is completed with any success. _____ There is little, if any, evidence that the student understands key concepts and procedures. _____ Student work and explanations are very difficult to follow and may be incomprehensible. _____ Any additional illustrations, if present, do not enhance communication and are irrelevant. _____ Answers to all parts are incorrect.

PERFORMANCE ASSESSMENT

Football Digits

Purpose
To assess student performance after completing Chapters 1–8.

Materials
none

Time
10 to 15 minutes per task

Grouping
Individuals or partners

Overview
Explain to students that this performance assessment is about football.
Each task is about a situation related to a football stadium or football tickets.

Task A-1   Will I Get a Seat?
Students are asked to look at a diagram of a football stadium and use the information given about the number of seats in one section to estimate the number in another section and the number of seats in the whole stadium.

Task A-2   Making Big Bucks
Students are given the price of a football ticket and are asked to find the ticket sales for a section of the stadium that is half empty. Then they are asked to find the number of tickets that must be sold to generate $45,000.

Task A-3   Lots of Work
Students are asked to estimate what it costs to maintain food stands at a stadium, given the cost of maintaining the stadium and the relationship between that cost and the cost of maintaining the food stands. Then they are asked to complete a table of the stadium's operating costs per month.

Task A-4   Fans Flood the Stadium
Students are asked to determine the number of shuttle buses that will be needed to transport fans from the parking lot to the stadium, given on the number of people who can ride on a bus, the number of hours the buses will run, and the amount of time it takes a bus to make a round-trip.

Name _____ Date _____

Football Digits

Task	Performance Indicators	Observations and Rubric Score (One score per task)
A-1	_____ Determines that the area of section A is about 6 times as large as the area of section C. _____ Uses the relationship between the areas of sections A and C to estimate the number of seats in section C. _____ Estimates that there are about 3,300 seats in section C. _____ Estimates that the stadium seats about 15,400 people. _____ Explains that there will be enough seats for 14,000 people because 14,000 is less than 15,400.	3 2 1 0
A-2	_____ Determines that there are fans in one half of the 800 seats, or in 400 seats. _____ Explains that the ticket sales in the special section for Saturday's game will be 400 × $75, or $30,000. _____ Explains that $45,000 ÷ $75, or 600 tickets need to be sold to generate $45,000 in ticket sales.	3 2 1 0
A-3	_____ Multiplies $40,000 by $2\frac{1}{2}$ to estimate what it costs to maintain the food stands. _____ Subtracts to find about how much more it costs to maintain the food stands than the stadium. _____ Completes the table to show a total cost of $9,000,000 to operate the stadium for 12 months. _____ Identifies the costs for 6 months as $1,000,000, the costs for 4 months as more than $200,000, and the costs for 2 months as less than $100,000. _____ Explains how these costs were determined.	3 2 1 0
A-4	_____ Identifies 24 as the number of trips one bus can make in 4 hours. _____ Multiplies 66 by 24 to find the number of people one bus can transport in 4 hours. _____ Divides 70,000 by 1,584 to find the number of buses needed.	3 2 1 0
	Total Score _____/12	

Will I Get a Seat?

Super Star Stadium

Star School has a football game soon.
The picture shows a diagram of the
stadium. The stadium seats 550
people in section A.

Estimate how many seats are in section C.

_____

```
        B            D
     A      C      E
     R             F
       Q    ┌──────┐ G
     P      │50 yd │ H
       O    │ line │
            └──────┘
     N  M            K  J
            L
```

Show your work and explain.

At the next football game 14,000 people are expected.
Will there be enough seats? Explain why or why not.

_____

_____

_____

_____

Show the work you did to find if there will be enough seats.

Making Big Bucks

The special section at Championship Stadium gives fans the best view of the football game. This section usually holds 800 fans.

Suppose that half of the special section is left empty for Saturday's game. What will the ticket sales be if the tickets are sold for $75 each?

_____

> **Show your work and explain.**

The team owners decide that the ticket sales need to be at least $45,000. How many tickets need to be sold?

_____

> **Show your work and explain.**

Lots of Work

A football stadium needs a lot of work.

It costs $39,780 each month to maintain the stadium. The food stands cost about $2\frac{1}{2}$ times as much to run each month as the stadium.

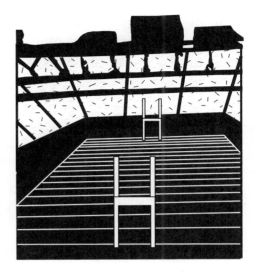

Estimate what it costs to maintain the food stands each month. _____

About how much more does it cost to maintain the food stands than the stadium each month? _____

Show and label your work. Explain your answer.

The total cost to operate the football stadium for 12 months is about $9,000,000. For 6 months of the year, the cost is $1,000,000 a month. For 4 months of the year the cost is more than $200,000 a month. The remaining months cost less than $100,000. What are the operating costs for each of the 12 months? Fill in the table with the costs. Explain your thinking and show how you got these costs.

_____

_____

_____

Month	Cost

Fans Flood the Stadium

The newspaper predicts that 70,000 people will attend Saturday's big play-off game. The plan is to take fans from the parking lot to the stadium by using shuttle buses.

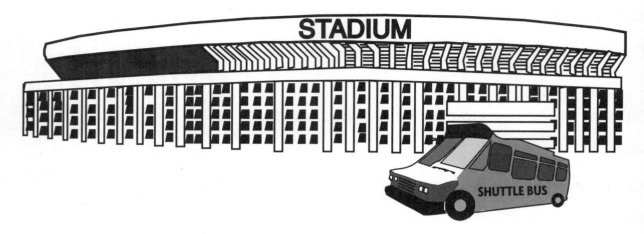

For safety reasons, each shuttle bus can transport only 66 people at a time. These buses will start service 4 hours before the game. A round trip to the stadium and back to the parking lot takes 10 minutes.

How many shuttle buses are needed to make sure the fans get to

the game on time? _____

Show the work you did to find how many buses are needed. Explain.

Reduced and Annotated Pupil Pages for
Football Digits

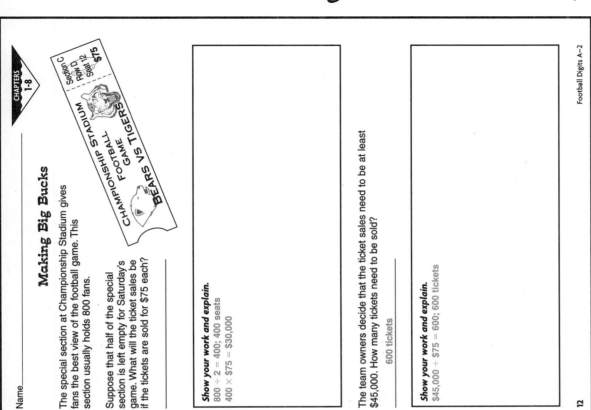

Name _____

Making Big Bucks

The special section at Championship Stadium gives fans the best view of the football game. This section usually holds 800 fans.

Suppose that half of the special section is left empty for Saturday's game. What will the ticket sales be if the tickets are sold for $75 each?

Show your work and explain.
800 ÷ 2 = 400; 400 seats
400 × $75 = $30,000

The team owners decide that the ticket sales need to be at least $45,000. How many tickets need to be sold?

600 tickets

Show your work and explain.
$45,000 ÷ $75 = 600; 600 tickets

Football Digits A–2

12

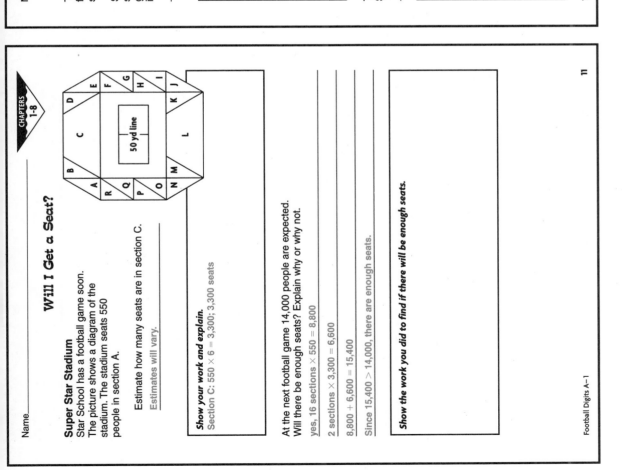

Name _____

Will I Get a Seat?

Super Star Stadium
Star School has a football game soon. The picture shows a diagram of the stadium. The stadium seats 550 people in section A.

Estimate how many seats are in section C.
Estimates will vary.

Show your work and explain.
Section C: 550 × 6 = 3,300; 3,300 seats

At the next football game 14,000 people are expected. Will there be enough seats? Explain why or why not.

yes, 16 sections × 550 = 8,800

2 sections × 3,300 = 6,600

8,800 + 6,600 = 15,400

Since 15,400 > 14,000, there are enough seats.

Show the work you did to find if there will be enough seats.

Football Digits A–1

11

CHAPTERS
1-8

Name _____

Fans Flood the Stadium

The newspaper predicts that 70,000 people will attend Saturday's big play-off game. The plan is to take fans from the parking lot to the stadium by using shuttle buses.

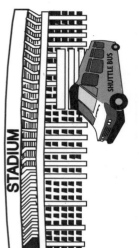

STADIUM

SHUTTLE BUS

For safety reasons, each shuttle bus can transport only 66 people at a time. These buses will start service 4 hours before the game. A round trip to the stadium and back to the parking lot takes 10 minutes.

How many shuttle buses are needed to make sure the fans get to the game on time? _____ about 45 buses

Show the work you did to find how many buses are needed. Explain.

70,000 ÷ 66 = 1,060.6, or 1,061 bus trips

6 trips per hour × 4 hr = 24 trips

1,061 ÷ 24 = 44.21; about 45 buses are needed.

Note: Some students may assume that some time is needed to get into the stadium and get settled. Consequently, the student could use $3\frac{3}{4}$ hours as the amount of time the shuttle buses need.

14

Football Digits A–4

CHAPTERS
1-8

Name _____

Lots of Work

A football stadium needs a lot of work.

It costs $39,780 each month to maintain the stadium. The food stands cost about $2\frac{1}{2}$ times as much to run each month as the stadium.

Estimate what it costs to maintain the food stands each month. _____ about $100,000

About how much more does it cost to maintain the food stands than the stadium each month? _____ about $60,000

Show and label your work. Explain your answer.
Explanations will vary.

The total cost to operate the football stadium for 12 months is about $9,000,000. For 6 months of the year, the cost is $1,000,000 a month. For 4 months of the year the cost is more than $200,000 a month. The remaining months cost less than $100,000. What are the operating costs for each of the 12 months? Fill in the table with the costs. Explain your thinking and show how you got these costs.

Possible answers:

Month	Cost
September	$1,000,000
October	$1,000,000
November	$1,000,000
December	$1,000,000
January	$1,000,000
February	$1,000,000
March	$705,000
April	$705,000
May	$705,000
June	$705,000
July	$90,000
August	$90,000

13

Football Digits A–3

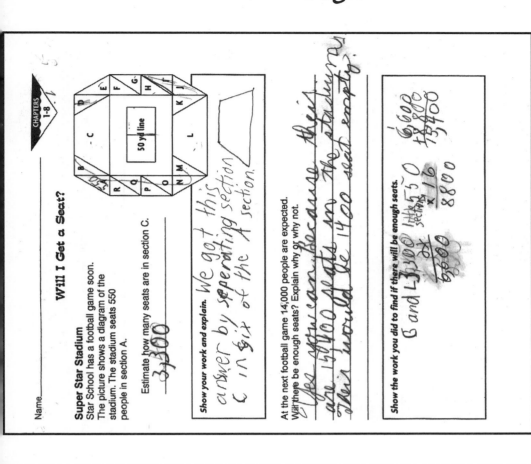

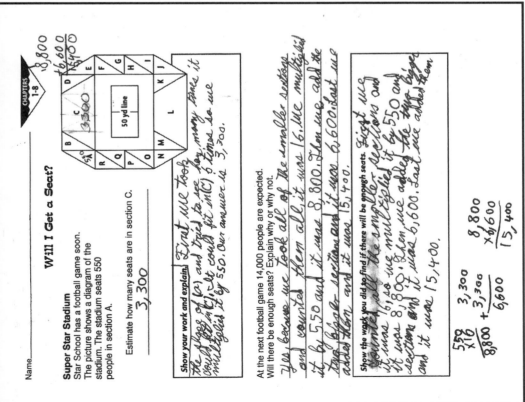

Level 2 The student successfully completed some of the parts. Other parts were attempted but not successfully completed. The student showed partial understanding of concepts. Additional illustrations did not enhance communication. Answers are correct for some parts but are partially correct for others.

Level 3 The student successfully completed all parts of the task. The student's work and explanations are clear. Answers for all parts are correct or reasonable.

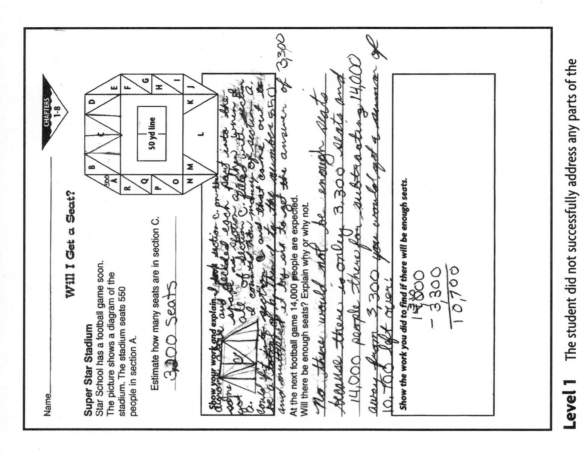

CHAPTERS 1-8

Name _____

Will I Get a Seat?

Super Star Stadium
Star School has a football game soon. The picture shows a diagram of the stadium. The stadium seats 550 people in section A.

Estimate how many seats are in section C.

___3,000 seats___

50 yd line

Show your work and explain. _I took section C and into the same as section A and divided section C into the same shape as section A. I counted the number of section A. could fit into section C and that came out to be 6. Then I found if by 6 to find if by or to get the number 550 and multiplied it by 6 to get the answer of 3300._

At the next football game 14,000 people are expected. Will there be enough seats? Explain why or why not.

No there would not be enough seats because there is only 3,300 seats and 14,000 people therefore subtracting 14,000 away from 3,300 you would get a answer of 10,700 left over.

Show the work you did to find if there will be enough seats.

$$\begin{array}{r} 13{,}000 \\ -\ 3{,}300 \\ \hline 10{,}700 \end{array}$$

Level 1 The student did not successfully address any parts of the task. The student shows a lack of understanding of concepts. The work is difficult to follow and requires you to fill in the gaps. Any additional illustrations do not enhance communication.

TEACHER NOTES

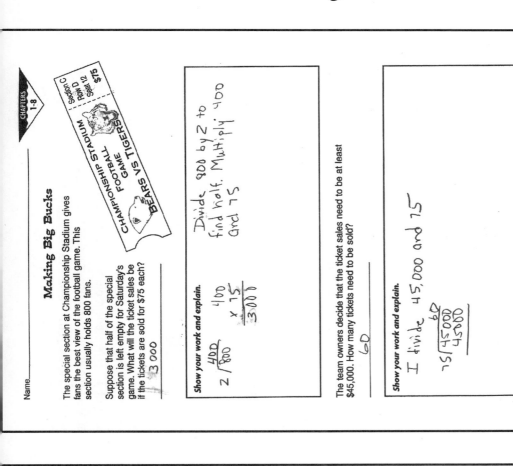

Making Big Bucks

Name_____

CHAPTERS 1-8

CHAMPIONSHIP STADIUM
FOOTBALL GAME
BEARS VS TIGERS
Section C
Row D
Seat 12
$75

The special section at Championship Stadium gives fans the best view of the football game. This section usually holds 800 fans.

Suppose that half of the special section is left empty for Saturday's game. What will the ticket sales be if the tickets are sold for $75 each?

3 000

Show your work and explain.

Divide 800 by 2 to
find half. Multiply 400
and 75

400
2)800

400
x 15
3000

The team owners decide that the ticket sales need to be at least $45,000. How many tickets need to be sold?

Show your work and explain.

I divide 45,000 and 75

60
75)45,000
45,000

Level 2 The student attempted but not successfully completed. The parts were attempted but not successfully completed. The student shows partial understanding of concepts. Answers are correct for some parts but are partially correct or incorrect for others.

Making Big Bucks

Name_____

CHAPTERS 1-8

CHAMPIONSHIP STADIUM
FOOTBALL GAME
BEARS VS TIGERS
Section C
Row D
Seat 12
$75

The special section at Championship Stadium gives fans the best view of the football game. This section usually holds 800 fans.

Suppose that half of the special section is left empty for Saturday's game. What will the ticket sales be if the tickets are sold for $75 each?

3000

Show your work and explain.

Half of 800 is 400 so I
multiplyed 400 by 45 and
I got 30,000.
To get 400 I divided
800 by 2 and got 400.

$800 \div 2 = 400$

The team owners decide that the ticket sales need to be at least $45,000. How many tickets need to be sold?

Show your work and explain.

I got 600 by dividing
75 into 45,000. And
I divided 45 into
45,000 because I
wanted to find out how
many tickets needed to
be sold.

600
75)45,000

Level 3 The student successfully completed all parts of the task. The intents of all parts of the task were addressed with appropriate strategies and procedures. The student's work and explanations are clear. Answers for all parts are correct.

Model Student Papers for
Football Digits

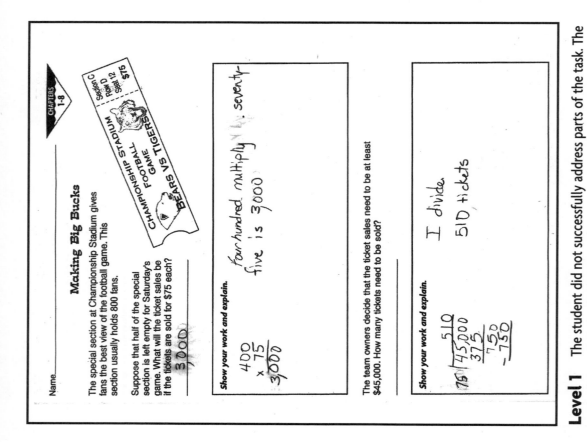

TEACHER NOTES

Level 1 The student did not successfully address parts of the task. The student shows a lack of understanding of concepts. Student work requires you to fill in the gaps. Answers to most parts are incorrect.

Top student paper (Level 2)

Name _____

CHAPTERS 1-8

Lots of Work

A football stadium needs a lot of work.

It costs $39,780 each month to maintain the stadium. The food stands cost about $2\frac{1}{2}$ times as much to run each month as the stadium.

Estimate what it costs to maintain the food stands each month. $100,500

About how much more does it cost to maintain the food stands than the stadium each month? $9,950

Show and label your work. Explain your answer.
(handwritten) I had to multiply $39,780 2½ times more and saw got $9,950. Then ½ because the food stand more got $9,950.

Month	Cost
January	1,000,000
February	7,000,000
March	1,000,000
April	1,000,000
May	1,000,000
June	
July	1,250,000
August	250,000
September	75,000
October	650,000
November	300,000
December	300,000

The total cost to operate the football stadium for 12 months is about $9,000,000. For 6 months of the year, the cost is $1,000,000 a month. For 4 months of the year the cost is more than $200,000 a month. The remaining months cost less than $100,000. What are the operating costs for each of the 12 months? Fill in the table with the costs. Explain your thinking and show how you got these costs.

Level 2 The student successfully completed some of the parts. Other parts were attempted but not successfully completed, as in estimating. The student shows partial understanding of concepts. Explanations were not made, and inferences need to be made to understand the response. Answers are correct for some parts but are incorrect for others.

Bottom student paper (Level 3)

Name _____

CHAPTERS 1-8

Lots of Work

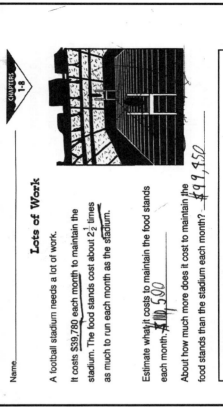

A football stadium needs a lot of work.

It costs $39,780 each month to maintain the stadium. The food stands cost about $2\frac{1}{2}$ times as much to run each month as the stadium.

Estimate what it costs to maintain the food stands each month. about $100,000

About how much more does it cost to maintain the food stands than the stadium each month? about $60,000

Show and label your work. Explain your answer.
Round $39,780 to $40,000. Multiply $40,000. Change $2\frac{1}{2}$ to 2.5. Subtract $100,000 and $40,000.

$40,000 to $40,000 and 2.5.
$40,000
× 2.5
———
100,000

100,000
− 40,000
———
60,000

Month	Cost
January	1,000,000
February	1,005,000
March	1,000,000
April	1,000,000
May	1,000,000
June	1,000,000
July	60,000
August	50,000
September	722,500
October	722,500
November	722,500
December	722,500

The total cost to operate the football stadium for 12 months is about $9,000,000. For 6 months of the year, the cost is $1,000,000 a month. For 4 months of the year the cost is more than $200,000 a month. The remaining months cost less than $100,000. What are the operating costs for each of the 12 months? Fill in the table with the costs. Explain your thinking and show how you got these costs.

First I put down six 1 millions. Then I put down 60,000 and 50,000 since they are less than 100,000. I added the six 1 millions, 60,000 and 50,000 to get 2,890,000. I divided 2,890,000 by 4 and got 722,500. I used 722,500 for the last 4 months.

Football Digits A–3

Level 3 The student successfully completed all or most parts of the task. The intents of all parts of the task were addressed with appropriate strategies and procedures. The student's work and explanations are clear. Answers for all parts are correct.

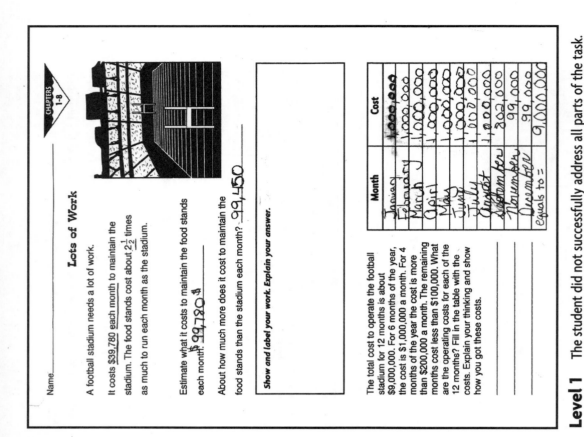

CHAPTERS 1-8

Name _____

Lots of Work

A football stadium needs a lot of work.

It costs $39,780 each month to maintain the stadium. The food stands cost about $2\frac{1}{2}$ times as much to run each month as the stadium.

Estimate what it costs to maintain the food stands each month: $99,780 ? $99,450

About how much more does it cost to maintain the food stands than the stadium each month? 99,450

Show and label your work. Explain your answer.

The total cost to operate the football stadium for 12 months is about $9,000,000. For 6 months of the year, the cost is $1,000,000 a month. For 4 months of the year the cost is more than $200,000 a month. The remaining months cost less than $100,000. What are the operating costs for each of the 12 months? Fill in the table with the costs. Explain your thinking and show how you got these costs.

Month	Cost
January	1,000,000
February	1,000,000
March	1,000,000
April	1,000,000
May	1,000,000
June	1,000,000
July	1,000,000
August	1,000,000
September	202,000
November	99,000
December	99,000
equals to =	9,000,000

TEACHER NOTES

Level 1 The student did not successfully address all parts of the task. There is limited evidence that the student understands concepts and procedures. The student's work is difficult to follow and requires you to fill in gaps to understand the response. There is no explanation of how the student arrived at the solution.

Level 2 paper

CHAPTERS 1-8

Name _____

Fans Flood the Stadium

The newspaper predicts that 70,000 people will attend Saturday's big play-off game. The plan is to take fans from the parking lot to the stadium by using shuttle buses.

STADIUM

SHUTTLE BUS

For safety reasons, each shuttle bus can transport only 66 people at a time. These buses will start service 4 hours before the game. A round trip to the stadium and back to the parking lot takes 10 minutes.

How many shuttle buses are needed to make sure the fans get to

the game on time? ___45___

Show the work you did to find how many buses are needed. Explain.

$60 \div 10 = 6 \times 4 = 24 \times 66 = 1584$ $70,000 \div 1584 = 44.19$

There's no such thing as a field of a

bus so we say 45.

First we found how many trips the

bus can make in an hour and then we found how many

trips in four hours.

Level 2   The student successfully completed some of the parts. There is evidence that the student has an understanding of the task completed. Explanations were made, but inferences may need to be made to understand the responses. Answers are correct.

Level 3 paper

CHAPTERS 1-8

Name _____

Fans Flood the Stadium

The newspaper predicts that 70,000 people will attend Saturday's big play-off game. The plan is to take fans from the parking lot to the stadium by using shuttle buses.

STADIUM

SHUTTLE BUS

For safety reasons, each shuttle bus can transport only 66 people at a time. These buses will start service 4 hours before the game. A round trip to the stadium and back to the parking lot takes 10 minutes.

How many shuttle buses are needed to make sure the fans get to

the game on time? ___45 Buses___

Show the work you did to find how many buses are needed. Explain.

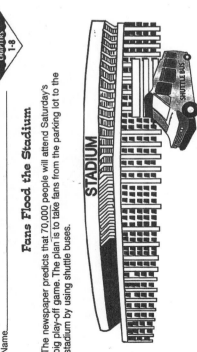

10 = 60 Each bus can take 6 round trips an hour. So each can take 24 round trips

6 × 4 = 24 in 4 hours. 24 round trips

24 × 66 = 1584 people each. This means 1584 people get transported in four hours.

70,000 ÷ 1584 = 45

45 buses are need to transport 70,000 People. The 45th bus is for the extra people.

Level 3   The student successfully completed all or most parts of the task. The intents of all parts of the task were addressed with a clear understanding of appropriate strategies and precedures. The student's work and explanations are clear and easy to follow. Answers for all parts are correct.

Model Student Papers for
Football Digits

Name _____

Fans Flood the Stadium

The newspaper predicts that 70,000 people will attend Saturday's big play-off game. The plan is to take fans from the parking lot to the stadium by using shuttle buses.

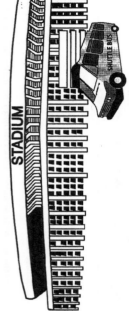

For safety reasons, each shuttle bus can transport only 66 people at a time. These buses will start service 4 hours before the game. A round trip to the stadium and back to the parking lot takes 10 minutes.

How many shuttle buses are needed to make sure the fans get to the game on time?

Show the work you did to find how many buses are needed. Explain.

First I figured out how many people can go on the bus at one hour. 660. Then I found out how many people can go on the bus in 4 hours is 2640. Then I divided 660 into 2640 and got 4. 4 is my answer

TEACHER NOTES

Level 1 The student did not successfully address parts of the task. There is limited evidence that the student understands concepts and procedures. The student's work is difficult to follow and requires you to fill in gaps to understand the response. Answers to most parts are incorrect.

Your Mouth

Purpose
To assess student performance after completing Chapters 9–14.

Materials
grid paper, stopwatch

Time
10 to 15 minutes per task

Grouping
Individuals or partners

Overview
Explain to students that this performance assessment is about mouths. Each task is related to your gums, your teeth, or your tongue.

Task B-1   Flossing Each Day Keeps the Dentist Away
Students are asked to determine the number of days one 5-meter roll of dental floss will last if 28 centimeters of dental floss is used every day. They are then asked to estimate the number of meters of floss that would be used by all the students in their class in one month.

Task B-2   Rolling Tongues
Students are asked to gather and organize data on the number of girls and the number of boys in the class who can roll their tongues in a U. They are then asked to use their data to predict how likely it is that a new boy enrolling in the class will be able to roll his tongue in a U.

Task B-3   How Many Teeth?
Students are asked to find out the ages of all the students in class and the number of permanent teeth each student has. They make a table to organize the data. They then determine the number of permanent teeth in each age group and the number of permanent teeth in the whole class.

Task B-4   Tired Tongues
Students are asked to see how many times they can stick out their tongues in 10 seconds. They repeat the 10-second test 10 times and use the data to make a graph. Then they find the mean, median, and mode.

Name _____ Date _____

Your Mouth

Task	Performance Indicators	Observations and Rubric Score (One score per task)
B-1	_____ Explains that there are 100 centimeters in 1 meter and 500 centimeters of floss in one 5-meter roll. _____ Divides 500 by 28 to determine how long a 5-meter roll of floss will last Annito. _____ Estimates the amount of floss the class would use in one month by multiplying the number of students in class × 28 cm × number of days in a month.	3 2 1 0
B-2	_____ Gathers data from all classmates. _____ Organizes the data so that it shows how many girls and how many boys can roll their tongues in a U-shape. _____ Uses the data to predict whether a new boy in the class is likely, certain, or unlikely to be able to roll his tongue. _____ Explains how the results of the survey were used to make the prediction.	3 2 1 0
B-3	_____ Finds out the ages and the numbers of permanent teeth for all the students in the class. _____ Organizes the data in a table. _____ Estimates the number of permanent teeth the students in each age group have. _____ Determines the total number of permanent teeth the students in the class have.	3 2 1 0
B-4	_____ Conducts the 10-second experiment 10 times and records the results. _____ Chooses an appropriate graph to display the data. _____ Makes the graph, including a title, labels, and a scale. _____ Finds the mean of the data. _____ Finds the median of the data. _____ Finds the mode of the data.	3 2 1 0

Total Score _____ /12

Flossing Each Day Keeps the Dentist Away

Flossing helps keep your gums healthy. Annito flosses her teeth every day.

Annito uses 28 centimeters of dental floss each day. Floss comes in 5-meter rolls. How many days

will one roll last Annito? _____

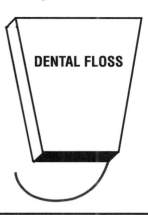

DENTAL FLOSS

Show your work and label so that how you got your answer is clear.

Suppose each student in your class uses as much floss a day as Annito. Estimate how many meters of floss your class would use in

one month. _____

Show your work and label so that how you got your answer is clear.

Rolling Tongues

You want to find out how many students in your class can roll their tongues in a U-shape. You also want to know if there is a difference between the numbers of girls and boys who can roll their tongues. Gather data from all of your classmates.

Organize your data to show what you find out.

Suppose a new boy enrolls in your class. Is it likely, certain, or unlikely that he will be able to roll his tongue in a U-shape?

_____

Explain your answer.

_____

_____

_____

How Many Teeth?

Your permanent teeth appear in your mouth at different ages.
The chart below shows at what age to expect them to appear.

Age	Permanent Teeth That Have Appeared
6–7 years	4 first molars
6–8 years	4 central incisors
7–9 years	4 lateral incisors
9–12 years	4 canines
10–12 years	4 second molars 8 bicuspids
16–25 years	4 wisdom teeth

Find out the ages of all students in your class and the number of permanant teeth each student has. Make a table to organize and show the data. Don't forget to include yourself.

Ages	Number of Students	Total Number of Permanent Teeth

About how many permanent teeth do the students in each age group have? Use the information from the table to make your estimates. Then put the numbers in your table.

Show your work and label it.

How many teeth in the whole class?

_____

_____

Tired Tongues!

Record how many times you can stick out your tongue in 10 seconds. Repeat this 10-second test 15 times. Use a stopwatch or a clock to time yourself.

Make a graph below to show your data.

Find the mean, median, and mode of the number of times you can stick out your tongue.

Mean: _____   Median: _____   Mode: _____

Show how you found these measures. Explain.

Name _____

Rolling Tongues

You want to find out how many students in your class can roll their tongues in a U-shape. You also want to know if there is a difference between the numbers of girls and boys who can roll their tongues. Gather data from all of your classmates.

Organize your data to show what you find out.

Possible Answer:

U-Shape Tongue Roll
Boys ### ### ### ///
Girls ### ### //

Possible graph:

U-Shape Tongue Rolls

Boys
Girls

0 2 4 6 8 10 12 14 16 18 20

Suppose a new boy enrolls in your class. Is it likely, certain, or unlikely that he will be able to roll his tongue in a U-shape?

Explain your answer.
Answers will vary depending on class graph.

28

Your Mouth B–2

Name _____

Flossing Each Day Keeps the Dentist Away

DENTAL FLOSS

Flossing helps keep your gums healthy. Annito flosses her teeth every day.

Annito uses 28 centimeters of dental floss each day. Floss comes in 5-meter rolls. How many days will one roll last Annito? _____ **about 17 days**

Show your work and label so that how you got your answer is clear.

5 m = 500 cm
500 cm ÷ 28 = 17.85, or 17 days

Suppose each student in your class uses as much floss a day as Annito. Estimate how many meters of floss your class would use in one month. _____ **Possible answer: about 252 m per month**

Show your work and label so that how you got your answer is clear.

Answers will vary depending on number of days in month used and number of students in the class.

Possible answer: 30 students × 28 cm = 840 cm or 8.4 m per day
30 days per mon × 28 cm = 840 cm
840 cm × 30 days = 25,200 cm, or 252 m per month

27

Your Mouth B–1

CHAPTERS 9-14

Name _____

Tired Tongues!

Record how many times you can stick out your tongue in 10 seconds. Repeat this 10-second test 15 times. Use a stopwatch or a clock to time yourself.

Make a graph below to show your data.
Possible graph:

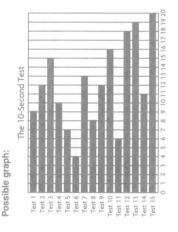

The 10-Second Test

Test 1
Test 2
Test 3
Test 4
Test 5
Test 6
Test 7
Test 8
Test 9
Test 10
Test 11
Test 12
Test 13
Test 14
Test 15

0 1 2 3 4 5 6 7 8 9 10 11 12 13 14 15 16 17 18 19 20

Find the mean, median, and mode of the number of times you can stick out your tongue. Answers based on sample data.

Mean: ____12____   Median: ____12____   Mode: ____12____

Show how you found these measures. Explain.

4, 6, 7, 8, 9, 10, 11, 12, 12, 13, 15, 16, 18, 19, 20
                    ↑   ↑
                  mode   median

$4 + 6 + 7 + 8 + 9 + 10 + 11 + 12 + 12 + 13 + 15 + 16 + 18 + 19 + 20 = 180$
$180 \div 15 = 12$

30

Your Mouth B–4

CHAPTERS 9-14

Name _____

How Many Teeth?

Your permanent teeth appear in your mouth at different ages. The chart below shows at what age to expect them to appear.

Age	Permanent Teeth That Have Appeared
6–7 years	4 first molars
6–8 years	4 central incisors
7–9 years	4 lateral incisors
9–12 years	4 canines
10–12 years	4 second molars
	8 bicuspids
16–25 years	4 wisdom teeth

Find out the ages of all students in your class and the number of permanent teeth each student has. Make a table to organize and show the data. Don't forget to include yourself.
Possible answers:

Ages	Number of Students	Total Number of Permanent Teeth
9 yr	3 students × 16 teeth	about 48 teeth
10 yr	15 students × 28 teeth	about 420 teeth
11 yr	12 students × 28 teeth	about 336 teeth

About how many permanent teeth do the students in each age group have? Use the information from the table to make your estimates. Then put the numbers in your table.

Show your work and label it.

How many teeth in the whole class? _____
Possible answer: 804 teeth

Your Mouth B–3

29

Left paper (Level 3)

Name: _____

CHAPTERS 9-14

DENTAL FLOSS

Flossing Each Day Keeps the Dentist Away

Flossing helps keeps your gums healthy. Annito flosses her teeth every day.

Annito uses 28 centimeters of dental floss each day. Floss comes in 5-meter rolls. How many days will one roll last Annito? ___17___

Show your work and label so that how you got your answer is clear.

5 m = 500 cm

$$28\sqrt{500.00}$$

```
          17.85
28) 500.00
    28
    220
    176
    440
    224
    160
```

First I changed 5 meters to 500 centimeters
Then I divided 500 centimeters by 28 centimeters.
My answer is about 17.85 centimeters.
That means that one roll will last about 17 days.

Suppose each student in your class uses as much floss a day as Annito. Estimate how many meters of floss your class would use in one month. ___24,000___

Show your work and label so that how you got your answer is clear.

```
  28        784 ≈ 800
 x28        800
 224        x36
 56       24,000
 784
```

There are 28 students in my class.
I multiplied 28 students and 28 centimeters of floss to get 784 centimeters of floss each day. I used 30 days in the month. I estimated 784 centimeters to 800 centimeters. I thru Multiplied 800 centimeters and 30 days.
I got 24,000 centimeters of floss.

Right paper (Level 2)

Name: _____

CHAPTERS 9-14

DENTAL FLOSS

Flossing Each Day Keeps the Dentist Away

Flossing helps keeps your gums healthy. Annito flosses her teeth every day.

Annito uses 28 centimeters of dental floss each day. Floss comes in 5-meter rolls. How many days will one roll last Annito? ___17___

Show your work and label so that how you got your answer is clear.

```
   28
   x 7
  196
```

```
28) 500
    28
```

divided 500 centimeters(inches) by 28 centimeters

Suppose each student in your class uses as much floss a day as Annito. Estimate how many meters of floss your class would use in one month. ___510___

Show your work and label so that how you got your answer is clear.

```
  17
 x30
  00
 510
 510
```

Multiply how many days it takes up x the days of the month

Level 2 The student successfully completed some of the parts. There is evidence that the student has partial understanding of key concepts and procedures. Some explanations were made, but inferences may need to be made to understand the responses. Answers are correct for some parts but are incorrect for others.

Level 3 The student successfully completed all or most parts of the task. The intents of all parts of the task were addressed with a clear understanding of appropriate strategies and procedures. The student's work and explanations are clear and easy to follow. Answers for all parts are correct.

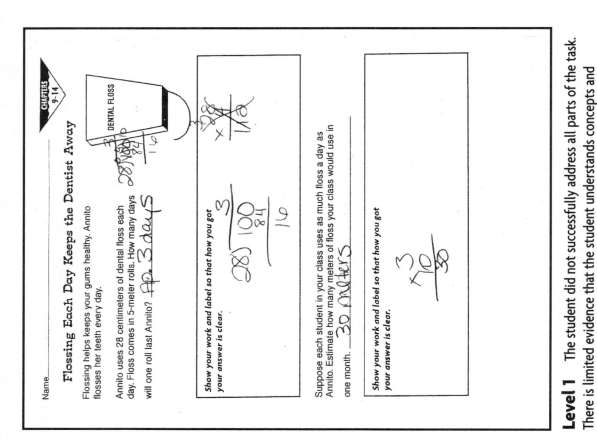

TEACHER NOTES

Level 1 The student did not successfully address all parts of the task. There is limited evidence that the student understands concepts and procedures. The student offered no explanations for the work done. Answers to most parts are incorrect.

Model Student Papers for
Your Mouth

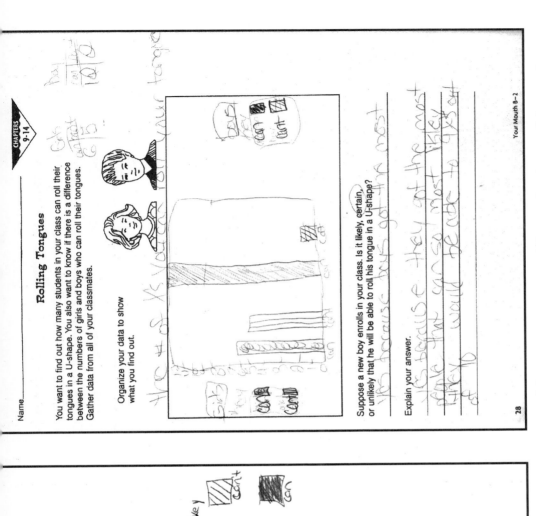

Rolling Tongues

Name _____

You want to find out how many students in your class can roll their tongues in a U-shape. You also want to know if there is a difference between the numbers of girls and boys who can roll their tongues. Gather data from all of your classmates.

Organize your data to show what you find out.

Suppose a new boy enrolls in your class. Is it likely, certain, or unlikely that he will be able to roll his tongue in a U-shape?

Explain your answer.

Most boys in our class were able to roll their tongue so I think the new boy would be able to roll his tongue

28

Your Mouth B-2

Level 3 The student successfully completed all or most parts of the task. The intents of all parts of the task were addressed with a clear understanding of appropriate strategies and procedures. The student's work and explanations are clear and easy to follow. Answers for all parts are correct.

Rolling Tongues

Name _____

You want to find out how many students in your class can roll their tongues in a U-shape. You also want to know if there is a difference between the numbers of girls and boys who can roll their tongues. Gather data from all of your classmates.

Organize your data to show what you find out.

Suppose a new boy enrolls in your class. Is it likely, certain, or unlikely that he will be able to roll his tongue in a U-shape?

Explain your answer.

28

Your Mouth B-2

Level 2 The student successfully completed some of the parts but not others. There is evidence that the student has partial understanding of how to make a bar graph. Some explanations were made, but inferences may need to be made to understand the responses. Answer are correct for some parts but are incorrect for others.

Model Student Papers for
Your Mouth

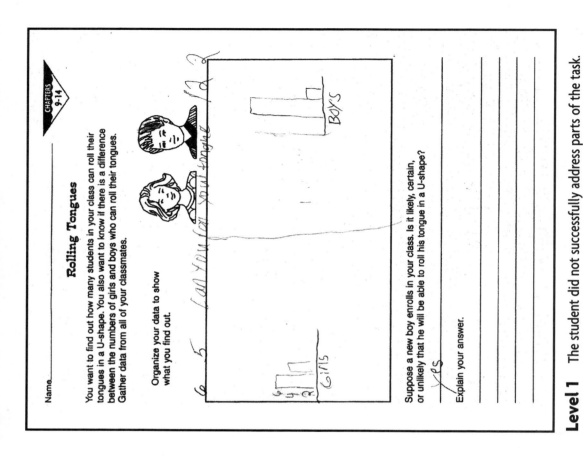

Rolling Tongues

Name _____

You want to find out how many students in your class can roll their tongues in a U-shape. You also want to know if there is a difference between the numbers of girls and boys who can roll their tongues. Gather data from all of your classmates.

Organize your data to show what you find out.

Suppose a new boy enrolls in your class. Is it likely, certain, or unlikely that he will be able to roll his tongue in a U-shape?

Explain your answer.

TEACHER NOTES

Level 1 The student did not successfully address parts of the task. There is limited evidence that the student understands concepts and procedures for making a graph. The student's work is difficult to follow. The student offered no explanations for the work done.

Model Student Papers for
Your Mouth

Name _____

How Many Teeth?

Your permanent teeth appear in your mouth at different ages.
The chart below shows at what age to expect them to appear.

Age	Permanent Teeth That Have Appeared
6–7 years	4 first molars
6–8 years	4 central incisors
7–9 years	4 lateral incisors
9–12 years	4 canines
10–12 years	4 second molars 8 bicuspids
16–25 years	4 wisdom teeth

Find out the ages of all students in your class and the number of permanent teeth each student has. Make a table to organize and show the data. Don't forget to include yourself.

Ages	Number of Students	Total Number of Permanent Teeth
11	12	
12	15	
13	1	

About how many permanent teeth do the students in each age group have? Use the information from the table to make your estimates. Then put the numbers in your table.

Show your work and label it.

How many teeth in the whole class?

759 teeth because I added all of the total number of teeth for the 3 ages.

Level 2   The student successfully completed some of the parts. There is evidence that the student has partial understanding of concepts and procedures. Some explanations were made, but inferences may need to be made to understand the responses. Answers are correct for some parts but are incorrect for others.

Name _____

How Many Teeth?

Your permanent teeth appear in your mouth at different ages.
The chart below shows at what age to expect them to appear.

Age	Permanent Teeth That Have Appeared
6–7 years	4 first molars
6–8 years	4 central incisors
7–9 years	4 lateral incisors
9–12 years	4 canines
10–12 years	4 second molars 8 bicuspids
16–25 years	4 wisdom teeth

Find out the ages of all students in your class and the number of permanent teeth each student has. Make a table to organize and show the data. Don't forget to include yourself.

Ages	Number of Students	Total Number of Permanent Teeth
11	18 x 17 teeth	
12	15 y 19 teeth	
13	1 x 21 teeth	

About how many permanent teeth do the students in each age group have? Use the information from the table to make your estimates. Then put the numbers in your table.

Show your work and label it.

How many teeth in the whole class?

Their is 510 teeth in the whole class.

Level 3   The student successfully completed all or most parts of the task. The intents of all parts of the task were addressed with a clear understanding of appropriate strategies and procedures. The student's work and explanations are clear and easy to follow. Answers for all parts are correct.

Model Student Papers for
Your Mouth

CHAPTERS 9-14

Name _____

How Many Teeth?

Your permanent teeth appear in your mouth at different ages.
The chart below shows at what age to expect them to appear.

Age	Permanent Teeth That Have Appeared
6–7 years	4 first molars
6–8 years	4 central incisors
7–9 years	4 lateral incisors
9–12 years	4 canines
10–12 years	4 second molars 8 bicuspids
16–25 years	4 wisdom teeth

Find out the ages of all students in your class and the number of permanent teeth each student has. Make a table to organize and show the data. Don't forget to include yourself.

Ages	Number of Students	Total Number of Permanent Teeth
11	15	20
12	11	20
13		6

About how many permanent teeth do the students in each age group have? Use the information from the table to make your estimates. Then put the numbers in your table.

Show your work and label it. Student 2 teeth 5 6 teeth
11-13 x 2 20 teeth
5 (teen)
2 08 3
teeth student that
(na) is thirteen

How many teeth in the whole class? _85 teeth_

TEACHER NOTES

Level 1 The student did not successfully address all parts of the task. There is limited evidence that the student understands the concept that the older a student is, the more teeth he or she should have. The student's work is difficult to follow and requires you to fill in gaps. The student offered no explanations for the work.

Model Student Papers for
Your Mouth

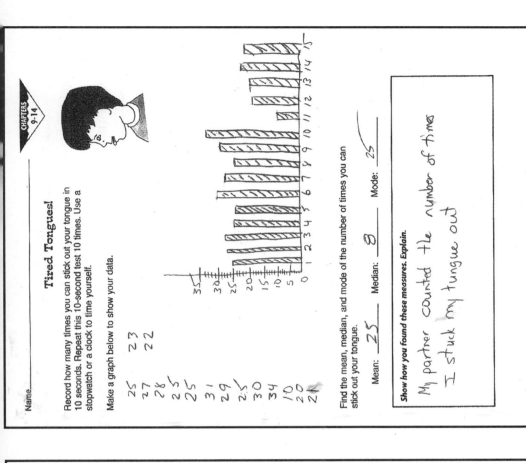

Tired Tongues!

Record how many times you can stick out your tongue in 10 seconds. Repeat this 10-second test 10 times. Use a stopwatch or a clock to time yourself.

Make a graph below to show your data.

45 37 38 32 35 36 33
31 43 44 47 42 25 34 13

Find the mean, median, and mode of the number of times you can stick out your tongue.

Mean: 31 Median: 34 Mode: 35

Show how you found these measures. Explain.

I found the mean by adding the number of times I could stick out my tongue in 10 seconds I divide by 15
I found the median by putting the numbers from least to highest, then I looked for the middle.
I found the mode by looking for the same numbers of times I sticked out my tongue in 10 seconds

Level 3 The student successfully completed all or most parts of the task. The intents of all parts of the task were addressed with a clear understanding of appropriate strategies and procedures. The student's work and explanations are clear and easy to follow. Answers for all or most parts are correct.

Tired Tongues!

Record how many times you can stick out your tongue in 10 seconds. Repeat this 10-second test 10 times. Use a stopwatch or a clock to time yourself.

Make a graph below to show your data.

25 23
27 36
28
25
25
31
29
26
30
34
10
20
21

Find the mean, median, and mode of the number of times you can stick out your tongue.

Mean: 25 Median: 8 Mode: 25

Show how you found these measures. Explain.

My partner counted the number of times I stick my tongue out

Level 2 The student successfully completed some of the parts. There is evidence that the student has partial understanding of concepts and procedures. Some explanations were made, but inferences may need to be made to understand the responses. Answers are correct for some parts but are partially correct or incorrect for others.

Model Student Papers for
Your Mouth

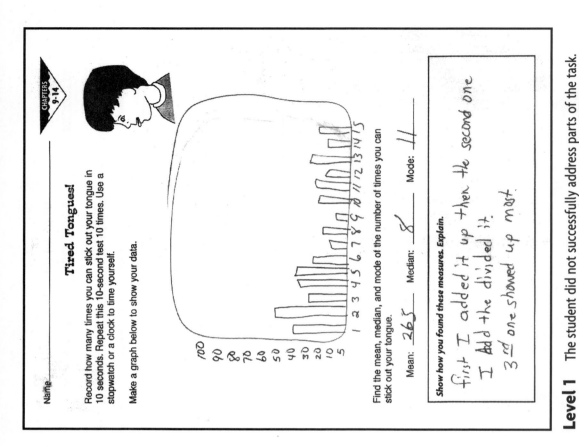

Tired Tongues!

Record how many times you can stick out your tongue in 10 seconds. Repeat this 10-second test 10 times. Use a stopwatch or a clock to time yourself.

Make a graph below to show your data.

100
90
80
70
60
50
40
30
20
10
5

1 2 3 4 5 6 7 8 9 10 11 12 13 14 15

Find the mean, median, and mode of the number of times you can stick out your tongue.

Mean: 265   Median: 8   Mode: 11

Show how you found these measures. Explain.

first I added it up then the second one
I Add the divided it.
3rd one showed up most

TEACHER NOTES

Level 1 The student did not successfully address parts of the task. There is limited evidence that the student understands concepts and procedures. The student's work is difficult to follow and requires you to fill in gaps. The student offered few explanations for the work.

Cookies

Purpose
To assess student performance after completing Chapters 15–22.

Materials
grid paper

Time
10 to 15 minutes per task

Grouping
Individuals or partners

Overview
Explain to students that this performance assessment is about cookies. Each task is about baking, selling, or sharing cookies

Task C-1   Cookies
Students are asked to determine how many batches of 5 dozen cookies they will need to make to have about 1,000 cookies. Then they are asked to determine how much of each ingredient they will need to make the cookies.

Task C-2   Cookies for Sale!
Students are asked to complete a table to show the number of boxes of cookies each of 5 classes sold, given the fractional part each class sold of the total number of boxes. They are then asked to make a graph to show the number of boxes of cookies each class sold.

Task C-3   Cookies Can Get You to the Aquarium!
Students are asked to think about what they need to know if they want to earn enough money selling cookies to cover the cost of a field trip for 28 students at $6 each. They decide how many cookies to sell and a price to charge for each cookie.

Task C-4   Double Peanut for Carrot Raisin
Students are asked to draw a diagram to show how various numbers of cookies can be divided evenly among 4 bakers. Then they are asked to determine whether given numbers of cookies can be divided evenly among 3 bags, 4 bags, 5 bags, and 6 bags.

Cookies

Task	Performance Indicators	Observations and Rubric Score (One score per task)
C-1	_____ Determines the number of dozens of cookies there are in 1,000 cookies. _____ Determines the number of batches of 5 dozen cookies that need to be made. _____ Determines how much of each ingredient is needed to make the cookies. _____ Shows work and explains how the answers were determined.	3 2 1 0
C-2	_____ Finds the number of boxes of cookies each class sold by finding the fractional part of 900 for each class. _____ Chooses an appropriate graph to display the data. _____ Makes the graph, including a title, labels, and scales.	3 2 1 0
C-3	_____ Determines the amount of money the class needs to earn to go to the aquarium. _____ Identifies a selling price for the cookies. _____ Determines how many cookies must be sold to make enough money for the trip. _____ Explains what Jose had to think about in order to decide on a price to charge for each cookie.	3 2 1 0
C-4	_____ Draws a diagram to show how 8 cookies, 12 cookies, 6 cookies, and 4 cookies can be divided evenly among 4 people. _____ Determines whether 3 dozen cookies, 2 dozen cookies, 1 dozen cookies, and $1\frac{1}{2}$ dozen cookies can be divided evenly among 3 bags, 4 bags, 5 bags, and 6 bags. _____ Draws a diagram to show the different ways the cookies can be bagged evenly.	3 2 1 0

Total Score _____/12

Cookies

Your class wants to make cookies to raise money for a field trip. The recipe at the right makes 5 dozen cookies.

Recipe for Cookies	
$2\frac{1}{4}$ cups flour	$\frac{3}{4}$ cup packed brown sugar
1 tsp baking soda	1 tsp vanilla extract
1 tsp salt	2 eggs
1 cup butter	2 12-ounce packages of
$\frac{3}{4}$ cup granulated sugar	chocolate morsels
Makes 5 dozen cookies	

Your class wants to make about 1,000 cookies. How many dozens does your class

need to make? _____

How many batches of cookies are needed? _____

Show your work and explain.

Explain your thinking.

How much of each ingredient does your class need to make the cookies? Use your answer from part *a*. Show your work so that how you got your answers is clear.

Flour   _____

baking soda   _____

salt   _____

butter   _____

granulated sugar _____

brown sugar   _____

vanilla extract _____

eggs   _____

chocolate morsels _____

Show your work.

Cookies for Sale!

The fifth-grade classes had a bake sale
to raise money.

They sold a total of 900 boxes of cookies.
How many boxes of cookies did each
class sell? Complete the table below.

Class	Mrs. Snipes	Mrs. Huynh	Mr. Hondas	Mrs. Amick	Mr. Gunther
Fraction Sold	$\frac{1}{6}$	$\frac{1}{3}$	$\frac{1}{12}$	$\frac{1}{4}$	$\frac{1}{6}$
Boxes of Cookies Sold					

Total 900 boxes

*Show how you figured out the number of boxes of
cookies sold. Label your work.*

Make a graph to show how many boxes of cookies each class sold.
Be sure to title and label your graph.

Cookies Can Get You to the Aquarium!

The fifth grade at Jose's school is going to the Aquarium.

Tickets to the aquarium cost $6 for each student. There are 28 students in Jose's class. The school cafeteria has volunteered to bake cookies for the class to sell. All the money raised will go to pay for the trip. Jose's teacher asked him to figure out how many cookies the class needs to sell.

Think about what Jose needs to know. Then tell the cafeteria how many cookies to bake.

How many cookies should Jose tell the cafeteria to bake?

_____

Show the work you did to estimate the total number of cookies to bake.

Explain what Jose had to think about in order to decide on a price to charge for each cookie sold.

_____

_____

_____

_____

_____

Double Peanut Butter for Carrot Raisin

There are 4 bakers in your community who have a monthly cookie exchange.

One baker brought 8 nut cookies. Another baker brought 12 peanut cookies. A third baker brought 6 carrot-raisin cookies, and a fourth baker brought 4 toffee cookies. How can each bag of cookies be divided evenly among the 4 bakers?

Draw a diagram of how you would divide the cookies in each bag.

This month the bakers brought these cookies to exchange.

Baker	Amount of Cookies	Kind of Cookie
Betty Baker	3 dozen	Nut
Barney Batter	2 dozen	Peanut
Samuel Spatula	1 dozen	Carrot-raisin
Diane Dough	$1\frac{1}{2}$ dozen	Toffee

The bakers divide their cookies evenly in plastic bags. Each bag will contain the same number of each kind of cookies. Can the bakers

divide the cookies evenly by using 3 bags? _____ 4 bags? _____

5 bags? _____ 6 bags? _____

      Example: Using 2 bags, each bag would contain these cookies.
- 18 Nut
- 12 Peanut
- 6 Carrot-raisin
- 9 Toffee

Show the different ways that the cookies can be bagged evenly.

Name _____

Cookies for Sale!

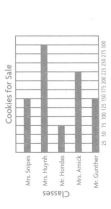

The fifth-grade classes had a bake sale to raise money.

They sold a total of 900 boxes of cookies. How many boxes of cookies did each class sell? Complete the table below.

Class	Mrs. Snipes	Mrs. Huynh	Mr. Hondas	Mrs. Amick	Mr. Gunther
Fraction Sold	$\frac{1}{6}$	$\frac{1}{3}$	$\frac{1}{12}$	$\frac{1}{4}$	$\frac{1}{6}$
Boxes of Cookies Sold	150 boxes	300 boxes	75 boxes	225 boxes	150 boxes

Total 900 boxes

Show how your figured out the number of boxes of cookies sold. Label your work.

$900 \div 3 = 300$ $900 \div 12 = 75$

$900 \div 6 = 150$ $900 \div 6 = 150$

$900 \div 4 = 225$

Make a graph to show how many boxes of cookies each class sold. Be sure to title and label your graph.

Possible graph:

Cookies for Sale

25 50 75 100 125 150 175 200 225 250 275 300

Classes — Mrs. Snipes, Mrs. Huynh, Mr. Hondas, Mrs. Amick, Mr. Gunther

44

Cookies C–2

Name _____

Cookies

Your class wants to make cookies to raise money for a field trip. The recipe at the right makes 5 dozen cookies.

Recipe for Cookies

$2\frac{1}{4}$ cup flour	$\frac{3}{4}$ cup packed brown sugar
1 tsp baking soda	1 tsp vanilla extract
1 tsp salt	2 eggs
1 cup butter	2 12-ounce packages of
$\frac{3}{4}$ cup granulated sugar	chocolate morsels

Makes 5 dozen cookies

Your class wants to make about 1,000 cookies. How many dozens does your class need to make? __about 84 doz__

How many batches of cookies are needed? __about 17__

Show your work and Explain.

$1,000 \div 12 = 83.3$, or about 84 doz $84 \div 5 = 16.8$, or about 17 batches.
Explain your thinking.

How much of each ingredient does your class need to make the cookies? Use your answer from part a. Show your work so that how you got your answers is clear. $83.3 \div 5 = 16.66$, or about 17 batches

Show your work.

flour	$2\frac{1}{4} \times 17$ batches $= 38\frac{1}{4}$ c
baking soda	1×17 batches $= 17$ tsp
salt	1×17 batches $= 17$ tsp
butter	1×17 batches $= 17$ c
granulated sugar	$\frac{3}{4} \times 17$ batches $= 12\frac{3}{4}$ c
brown sugar	$\frac{3}{4} \times 17$ batches $= 12\frac{3}{4}$ c
vanilla extract	1×17 batches $= 17$ tsp
eggs	2×17 batches $= 34$ eggs
chocolate morsels	2×17 batches $= 34$ 12-oz packages

43

Cookies C–1

CHAPTERS 15-22

Name _____

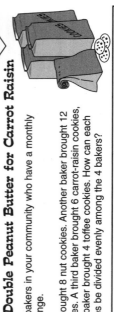

Double Peanut Butter for Carrot Raisin

There are 4 bakers in your community who have a monthly cookie exchange.

One baker brought 8 nut cookies. Another baker brought 12 peanut cookies. A third baker brought 6 carrot-raisin cookies, and a fourth baker brought 4 toffee cookies. How can each bag of cookies be divided evenly among the 4 bakers?

Draw a diagram of how you would divide the cookies in each bag.

nut
$8 \div 4 = 2$

peanut
$12 \div 4 = 3$

Carrot-raisin
$6 \div 4 = 1\frac{1}{2}$

toffee
$4 \div 4 = 1$

This month the bakers brought these cookies to exchange.

Baker	Amount of Cookies	Kind of Cookie
Betty Baker	3 dozen	Nut
Barney Batter	2 dozen	Peanut
Samuel Spatula	1 dozen	Carrot-raisin
Diane Dough	$1\frac{1}{2}$ dozen	Toffee

The bakers divide their cookies evenly in plastic bags. Each bag will contain the same number of each kind of cookies. Can the bakers divide the cookies evenly by using 3 bags? __yes__ 4 bags? __no__

5 bags? __no__ 6 bags? __yes__

Example: Using 2 bags, each bag would contain these cookies.
- 18 Nut
- 12 Peanut
- 6 Carrot-raisin
- 9 Toffee

Show the different ways that the cookies can be bagged evenly.

	2 bags	3 bags	6 bags
nut	18	12	6
peanut	12	8	4
Carrot-raisin	6	4	2
toffee	9	6	3

46

Cookies C-4

CHAPTERS 15-22

Name _____

Cookies Can Get You to the Aquarium!

The fifth grade at Jose's school is going to the Aquarium.

Tickets to the aquarium cost $6 for each student. There are 28 students in Jose's class. The school cafeteria has volunteered to bake cookies for the class to sell. All the money raised will go to pay for the trip. Jose's teacher asked him to figure out how many cookies the class needs to sell.

Think about what Jose needs to know. Then tell the cafeteria how many cookies to bake.

How many cookies should Jose tell the cafeteria to bake?

56 doz

Show the work you did to estimate the total number of cookies to bake.

$6 × 28 students = $168
If the cookies were sold for $0.25 each, the cafeteria would need to bake 672 cookies
$168 ÷ $0.25 = 672 cookies
672 cookies ÷ 12 = 56 doz

Explain what Jose had to think about in order to decide on a price to charge for each cookie sold.

Possible answer: the cost of each ticket, the total cost of the trip, how many students in the class, and how many cookies the cafeteria needed to bake

45

Cookies C-3

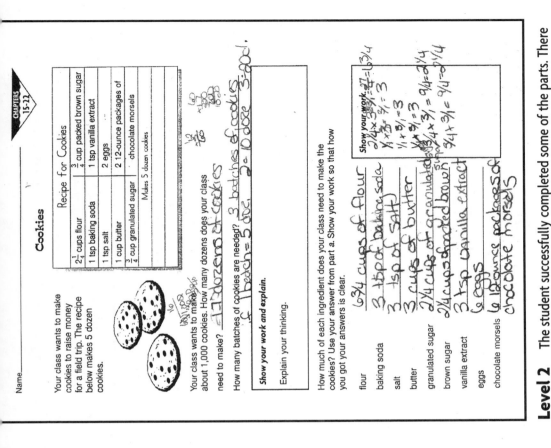

Name_____

Cookies

Your class wants to make cookies to raise money for a field trip. The recipe below makes 5 dozen cookies.

Recipe for Cookies

$2\frac{1}{4}$ cups flour	$\frac{3}{4}$ cup packed brown sugar
1 tsp baking soda	1 tsp vanilla extract
1 tsp salt	2 eggs
1 cup butter	2 12-ounce packages of chocolate morsels
$\frac{3}{4}$ cup granulated sugar	

Makes 5 dozen cookies

Your class wants to make about 1,000 cookies. How many dozens does your class need to make? 84 dozen

How many batches of cookies are needed? 17

Show your work and explain. I multiplied 12 x 84 = 1008 than I divided 8 into 84 because the recipe make 5dozencookies.

How much of each ingredient does your class need to make the cookies? Use your answer from part a. Show your work so that how you got your answers is clear.

flour	38 cups
baking soda	17 tsp
salt	17 tsp
butter	17 tsp
granulated sugar	15¼ cups
brown sugar	15¼ cups
vanilla extract	17 tsp
eggs	34 eggs
chocolate morsels	34 12ounce packages

Show your work.

$\frac{17}{1} \times 2\frac{1}{4} = \frac{9}{4} = \frac{153}{4} = \frac{153}{4}$

$\frac{3}{4} \times \frac{17}{1} = \frac{61}{4} = \frac{51}{4}$

Name_____

Cookies

Your class wants to make cookies to raise money for a field trip. The recipe below makes 5 dozen cookies.

Recipe for Cookies

$2\frac{1}{4}$ cups flour	$\frac{3}{4}$ cup packed brown sugar
1 tsp baking soda	1 tsp vanilla extract
1 tsp salt	2 eggs
1 cup butter	2 12-ounce packages of chocolate morsels
$\frac{3}{4}$ cup granulated sugar	

Makes 5 dozen cookies

Your class wants to make about 1,000 cookies. How many dozens does your class need to make? 17 dozens of cookies

How many batches of cookies are needed? 3 batches of cookies
1 batch = 5 doz, 3 = 10 doz = 3,000

Show your work and explain.

Explain your thinking.

How much of each ingredient does your class need to make the cookies? Use your answer from part a. Show your work so that how you got your answers is clear.

flour	6¾ cups of flour
baking soda	3 tsp of baking soda
salt	3 tsp of salt
butter	3 cups of butter
granulated sugar	2¼ cups of granulated
brown sugar	2¼ cups packed brown
vanilla extract	3 tsp vanilla extract
eggs	6 eggs
chocolate morsels	6 12-ounce packages of chocolate morsels

Show your work.

$2\frac{1}{4} \times 3 = \frac{27}{4} = 6\frac{3}{4}$

$1 \times 3 = \frac{9}{4}$

$1 \times 3 = 3$

$2\frac{1}{4} + 3 = \frac{9}{4} = 2\frac{1}{4}$

$\frac{3}{4} \times 3 = \frac{9}{4} = 2\frac{1}{4}$

Level 3 The student successfully completed all or most parts of the task. The intents of all parts of the task were addressed with a clear understanding of appropriate strategies and procedures. The student's work and explanations are clear and easy to follow. Answers for all or most parts are correct or reasonable but may be off because of minor errors, as in $\frac{3}{4} \times 17$.

Level 2 The student successfully completed some of the parts. There is evidence that the student has partial understanding of concepts and procedures. Explanations were made, but inferences may need to be made to understand the responses. Initially, the student divided by 60 instead of 12 making answers correct for some parts but partially correct or incorrect for others.

Model Student Papers for
Cookies

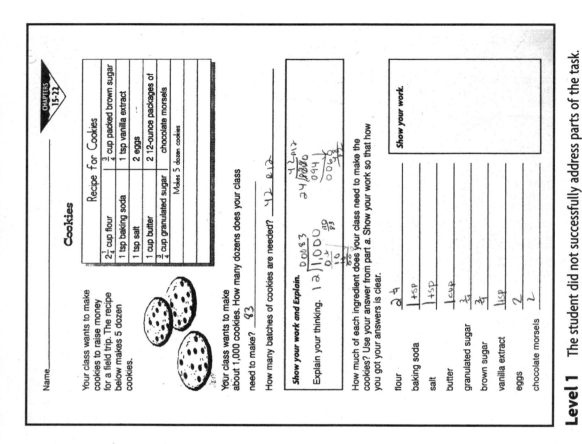

Name _____

Cookies

Your class wants to make cookies to raise money for a field trip. The recipe below makes 5 dozen cookies.

Recipe for Cookies

2¼ cup flour	¾ cup packed brown sugar
1 tsp baking soda	1 tsp vanilla extract
1 tsp salt	2 eggs
1 cup butter	2 12-ounce packages of
¾ cup granulated sugar	chocolate morsels

Makes 5 dozen cookies

Your class wants to make about 1,000 cookies. How many dozens does your class need to make? ___83___

How many batches of cookies are needed? ___42 R12___

Show your work and Explain.

Explain your thinking. 12) 1,000

How much of each ingredient does your class need to make the cookies? Use your answer from part a. Show your work so that how you got your answers is clear.

flour	2¼
baking soda	tsp
salt	tsp
butter	cup
granulated sugar	¾
brown sugar	¾
vanilla extract	tsp
eggs	2
chocolate morsels	2

Show your work.

Level 1
The student did not successfully address parts of the task. There is minimal or limited evidence that the student understands concepts and procedures. The student's work is difficult to follow and requires you to fill in gaps. The student offered no explanations for the work.

TEACHER NOTES

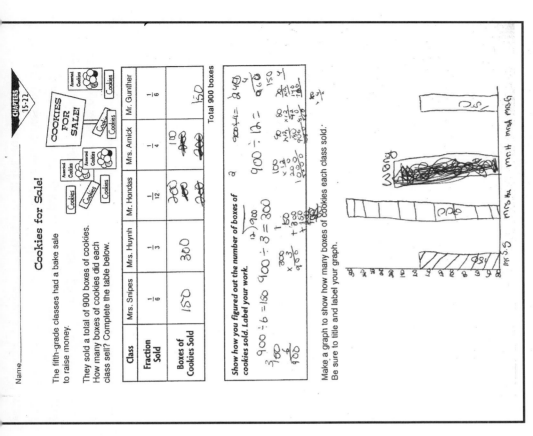

Name _____

Cookies for Sale!

The fifth-grade classes had a bake sale to raise money.

They sold a total of 900 boxes of cookies. How many boxes of cookies did each class sell? Complete the table below.

Class	Mrs. Snipes	Mrs. Huynh	Mr. Hondas	Mrs. Amick	Mr. Gunther
Fraction Sold	$\frac{1}{6}$	$\frac{1}{3}$	$\frac{1}{12}$	$\frac{1}{4}$	$\frac{1}{6}$
Boxes of Cookies Sold	150	300			150

Total 900 boxes

Show how you figured out the number of boxes of cookies sold. Label your work.

$900 \div 6 = 150$ $900 \div 3 = 300$

Make a graph to show how many boxes of cookies each class sold. Be sure to title and label your graph.

Level 2   The student successfully completed some of the parts. There is evidence that the student has partial understanding of concepts and procedures, such as in dividing 900 by 6 and in making a graph. Explanations were not made and inferences may need to be made to understand some responses. Answers are correct for some parts but are incorrect for others.

Name _____

Cookies for Sale!

The fifth-grade classes had a bake sale to raise money.

They sold a total of 900 boxes of cookies. How many boxes of cookies did each class sell? Complete the table below.

Class	Mrs. Snipes	Mrs. Huynh	Mr. Hondas	Mrs. Amick	Mr. Gunther
Fraction Sold	$\frac{1}{6}$	$\frac{1}{3}$	$\frac{1}{12}$	$\frac{1}{4}$	$\frac{1}{6}$
Boxes of Cookies Sold	150	300	75	225	150

Total 900 boxes

Show how you figured out the number of boxes of cookies sold. Label your work.

Example: 150
6)900   *Do this for each fraction (use denominator only when ÷) *then add all answers *total will be 900

Make a graph to show how many boxes of cookies each class sold. Be sure to title and label your graph.

Number of boxes of cookies sold in each class

Number of Boxes

Classes

Snipes   Huynh   Hondas   Amick   Gunther

Level 3   The student successfully completed all or most parts of the task. The intents of all parts of the task were addressed with a clear understanding of appropriate strategies and procedures. The student's work and explanations are clear and easy to follow. Answers for all parts are correct or reasonable.

Model Student Papers for
Cookies

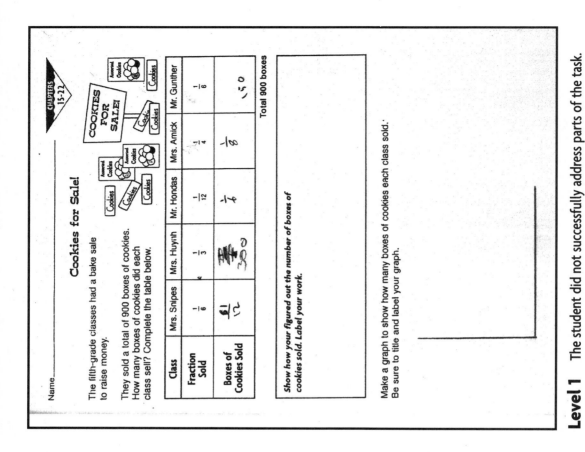

Cookies for Sale!

The fifth-grade classes had a bake sale to raise money.

They sold a total of 900 boxes of cookies. How many boxes of cookies did each class sell? Complete the table below.

Class	Mrs. Snipes	Mrs. Huynh	Mr. Hondas	Mrs. Amick	Mr. Gunther
Fraction Sold	$\frac{1}{6}$	$\frac{1}{3}$	$\frac{1}{12}$	$\frac{1}{4}$	$\frac{1}{6}$
Boxes of Cookies Sold	$\frac{6}{12}$	300	$\frac{1}{4}$	$\frac{1}{8}$	150

Total 900 boxes

Show how you figured out the number of boxes of cookies sold. Label your work.

Make a graph to show how many boxes of cookies each class sold. Be sure to title and label your graph.

Level 1 The student did not successfully address parts of the task. There is minimal or limited evidence that the student understands concepts and procedures, as in the division portion and the making of the graph. The student's work is difficult to follow and requires you to fill in gaps. The student offered no explanations for the work.

TEACHER NOTES

Cookies

Name _____

CHAPTERS 15-22

Cookies Can Get You to the Aquarium!

The fifth grade at Jose's school is going to the Aquarium.

Tickets to the aquarium cost $6 for each student. There are 28 students in Jose's class. The school cafeteria has volunteered to bake cookies for the class to sell. All the money raised will go to pay for the trip. Jose's teacher asked him to figure out how many cookies the class needs to sell.

Think about what Jose needs to know. Then tell the cafeteria how many cookies to bake.

How many cookies should Jose tell the cafeteria to bake?   444

Show the work you did to estimate the total number of cookies to bake.

2 per student
28 = 444 cookies
2 per child
should be sold

50¢ Per cookie

Explain what Jose had to think about in order to decide on a price to charge for each cookie sold.

50¢ per cookie
2 per child should be sold
2 per child
28 = 444 cookies

Level 2   The student successfully completed some of the parts. There is evidence that the student has partial understanding of concepts and procedures, as in the mistake in computation. Explanations were not made, and inferences may need to be made to understand the responses. Answers are correct for some parts but are incorrect for others.

Name _____

CHAPTERS 15-22

Cookies Can Get You to the Aquarium!

The fifth grade at Jose's school is going to the Aquarium.

Tickets to the aquarium cost $6 for each student. There are 28 students in Jose's class. The school cafeteria has volunteered to bake cookies for the class to sell. All the money raised will go to pay for the trip. Jose's teacher asked him to figure out how many cookies the class needs to sell.

Think about what Jose needs to know. Then tell the cafeteria how many cookies to bake.

How many cookies should Jose tell the cafeteria to bake? _____

Show the work you did to estimate the total number of cookies to bake.

28
x 6
$188

You should bake 188, charge $1.00 for each cookie, pay for the trip and have extra.

Explain what Jose had to think about in order to decide on a price to charge for each cookie sold.

He needed to know about how much money they needed in all. When he got that answer, he could tell how many cookies to bake and how much to sell them for.

Level 3   The student successfully completed all or most parts of the task. The intents of all parts of the task were addressed with a clear understanding of appropriate strategies and procedures. The student's work and explanations are clear and easy to follow. Answers for all parts are correct and reasonable but may be slightly off because of minor errors, as in 28 × 6.

Cookies C–3

TEACHER NOTES

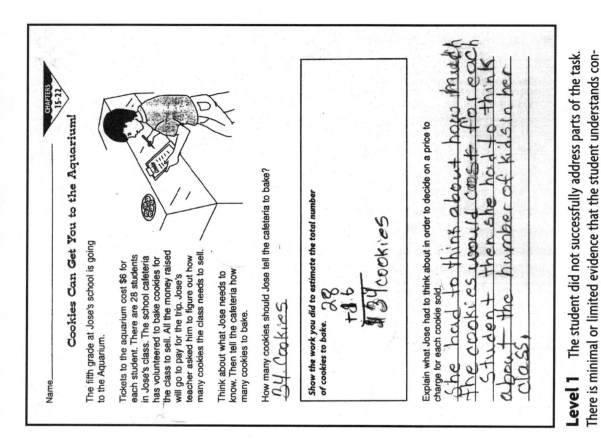

CHAPTERS
15-22

Cookies Can Get You to the Aquarium!

The fifth grade at Jose's school is going to the Aquarium.

Tickets to the aquarium cost $6 for each student. There are 28 students in Jose's class. The school cafeteria has volunteered to bake cookies for the class to sell. All the money raised will go to pay for the trip. Jose's teacher asked him to figure out how many cookies the class needs to sell.

Think about what Jose needs to know. Then tell the cafeteria how many cookies to bake.

How many cookies should Jose tell the cafeteria to bake?

By Cookies

Show the work you did to estimate the total number of cookies to bake.

28
+ 6
34 cookies

Explain what Jose had to think about in order to decide on a price to charge for each cookie sold.

She had to think about how much the cookies would cost for each student then she had to think about the number of kids in her class.

Level 1 The student did not successfully address parts of the task. There is minimal or limited evidence that the student understands concepts and procedures, as in the addition of 28 and 6, instead of multiplication. The student's work is difficult to follow and requires you to fill in gaps. The student offered few explanations for the work. Answers for most parts are incorrect.

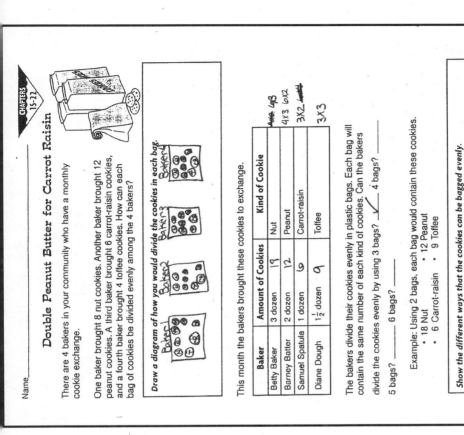

Name _____

CHAPTERS 15-22

Double Peanut Butter for Carrot Raisin

There are 4 bakers in your community who have a monthly cookie exchange.

One baker brought 8 nut cookies. Another baker brought 12 peanut cookies. A third baker brought 6 carrot-raisin cookies, and a fourth baker brought 4 toffee cookies. How can each bag of cookies be divided evenly among the 4 bakers?

Draw a diagram of how you would divide the cookies in each bag.

Baker1   Baker2   Baker3   Baker4

This month the bakers brought these cookies to exchange.

Baker	Amount of Cookies	Kind of Cookie	
Betty Baker	3 dozen	Nut	4×3 4p3
Barney Batter	2 dozen	Peanut	3X2 6x2
Samuel Spatula	1 dozen	Carrot-raisin	
Diane Dough	1½ dozen	Toffee	3×3

The bakers divide their cookies evenly in plastic bags. Each bag will contain the same number of each kind of cookies. Can the bakers divide the cookies evenly by using 3 bags? _____ 4 bags? ✓ _____

5 bags? _____ 6 bags? _____

Example: Using 2 bags, each bag would contain these cookies.
• 18 Nut   • 12 Peanut
• 6 Carrot-raisin   • 9 Toffee

Show the different ways that the cookies can be bagged evenly.

9 nut each
3 carrot-raisin each
6 peanut each
4½ Toffee each

Level 2
The student successfully completed some of the parts. There is evidence that the student has partial understanding of concepts and procedures, as in not showing all ways for the cookies to be divided. Explanations were not made and inferences may need to be made to understand the responses. Answers are correct for some parts but are incomplete for others.

Name _____

CHAPTERS 15-22

Double Peanut Butter for Carrot Raisin

There are 4 bakers in your community who have a monthly cookie exchange.

One baker brought 8 nut cookies. Another baker brought 12 peanut cookies. A third baker brought 6 carrot-raisin cookies, and a fourth baker brought 4 toffee cookies. How can each bag of cookies be divided evenly among the 4 bakers?

Draw a diagram of how you would divide the cookies in each bag.

I divided the number of cookies by 4

2 nut cookies in each bag, 3 peanut cookies, 1½ carrot-raisin cookies, and 1 toffee cookie

This month the bakers brought these cookies to exchange.

Baker	Amount of Cookies	Kind of Cookie
Betty Baker	3 dozen	Nut
Barney Batter	2 dozen	Peanut
Samuel Spatula	1 dozen	Carrot-raisin
Diane Dough	1½ dozen	Toffee

The bakers divide their cookies evenly in plastic bags. Each bag will contain the same number of each kind of cookies. Can the bakers divide the cookies evenly by using 3 bags? _____ 4 bags? ✓ _____

5 bags? _____ 6 bags? _____

Example: Using 2 bags, each bag would contain these cookies.
• 18 Nut   • 12 Peanut
• 6 Carrot-raisin   • 9 Toffee

Show the different ways that the cookies can be bagged evenly.

I divided the numbers of cookies by 6

6 nut in each, 4 peanut, 3 carrot, and 3 toffee

Level 3
The student successfully completed all or most parts of the task. The intents of all parts of the task were addressed with an understanding of appropriate strategies and procedures. The student's work and explanations are clear and easy to follow. Answers for all parts are correct but may be slightly off because of minor errors, as in showing all combinations.

Model Student Papers for
Cookies

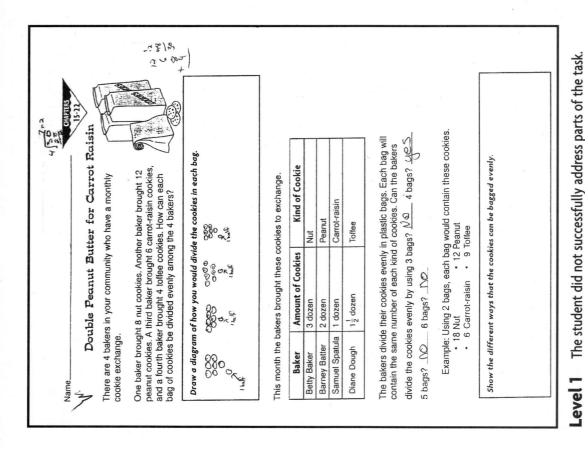

Double Peanut Butter for Carrot Raisin

Name _____

There are 4 bakers in your community who have a monthly cookie exchange.

One baker brought 8 nut cookies. Another baker brought 12 peanut cookies. A third baker brought 6 carrot-raisin cookies, and a fourth baker brought 4 toffee cookies. How can each bag of cookies be divided evenly among the 4 bakers?

Draw a diagram of how you would divide the cookies in each bag.

This month the bakers brought these cookies to exchange.

Baker	Amount of Cookies	Kind of Cookie
Betty Baker	3 dozen	Nut
Barney Batter	2 dozen	Peanut
Samuel Spatula	1 dozen	Carrot-raisin
Diane Dough	$1\frac{1}{2}$ dozen	Toffee

The bakers divide their cookies evenly in plastic bags. Each bag will contain the same number of each kind of cookies. Can the bakers divide the cookies evenly by using 3 bags? _No_ 4 bags? _yes_
5 bags? _No_ 6 bags? _No_

Example: Using 2 bags, each bag would contain these cookies.
- 18 Nut · 12 Peanut
- 6 Carrot-raisin · 9 Toffee

Show the different ways that the cookies can be bagged evenly.

TEACHER NOTES

Level 1 The student did not successfully address parts of the task. There is minimal or limited evidence that the student understands concepts and procedures. The student's work is difficult to follow and requires you to fill in gaps. The student offered no explanations for the work. Answers for most parts are incorrect.

T-Shirts

Purpose
To assess student performance after completing Chapters 23–28.

Materials
Circle divided into 10 equal sections for circle graph

Time
10 to 15 minutes per task

Grouping
Individuals or partners

Overview
Explain to students that this performance assessment is about T-shirts. Each task is about T-shirt designs or T-shirt sales.

Task D-1   T-Shirts Logo
Students are asked to design a logo for Math Club T-shirts that will fit in a specified bordered square on the shirts. The design must be a pattern of rectangles and squares inside the frame.

Task D-2   Cool T-Shirt Contest
Students are asked to complete a table by finding the percent of students in a school who entered a T-shirt contest. Then they determine how close this percent is to the goal of involving 90% of the students in the contest. Finally, they make a bar graph to compare the percents, and they explain what the graph shows.

Task D-3   Contest Rules
Students are asked to follow three rules while designing a 12-cm tessellation pattern for a T-shirt contest.

Task D-4   Order the Color You Want
Students are asked to make a circle graph to show the percent each color represents of the T-shirts sold. Then they find the ratio of blue T-shirts to black T-shirts and use the ratio to determine the number of blue shirts that will be sold if the ratio remains the same and the number of black shirts triples.

Name _____   Date _____

T-Shirts

Task	Performance Indicators	Observations and Rubric Score (One score per task)
D-1	_____ Determines the area of the inside square. _____ Determines the area of the outside square. _____ Draws a pattern of squares and rectangles that will fit inside the frame. _____ Identifies the number of squares and rectangles that fit inside the frame.	**3 2 1 0**
D-2	_____ Completes the table to show the percent of students who were in the contest. _____ Identifies the difference between 90% and the percent of students who are currently in the contest. _____ Makes a bar graph to show the percent of students who were in the contest for the past three years. _____ Explains what the graph shows.	**3 2 1 0**
D-3	_____ Makes a design that tessellates. _____ Makes a design that uses at least two regular polygons. _____ Makes a design that shows at least two lines of symmetry. _____ Makes a design that fits in a 12-cm square.	**3 2 1 0**
D-4	_____ Identifies the percent of each color of T-shirt that was sold last June. _____ Makes a circle graph, including a title and labels, to show the percent sold in each color. _____ Determines the ratio of blue shirts to black shirts. _____ Identifies the number of blue T-shirts they need to keep the ratio the same.	**3 2 1 0**

Total Score _____ /12

T-Shirts Logo

he Math Club is designing a new logo for its T-shirts. The design
ill have an 8 cm square with a 1 cm border around the square. An
utline of the new logo is shown.

Vhat is the area of the inside square?

_____

Vhat is the area of the outside square

_____

_____

he Math Club wants to use both 2-cm rectangles and 1-cm
quares to form a design inside the frame. Draw a design of blocks
hat will fit inside the frame. How many squares and rectangles will
t inside the frame?

Show and label your work.

Cool T-Shirt Contest

Every year the Math Club has a contest to see who can design the best Cool T-Shirt. The following table shows the number of students who were in the contest for the past three years.

When?	Number of Students in School	Students Who Were in the Contest	Percent of Students in Contest
Two years ago	800 students	160 students	
Last year	850 students	340 students	
This year	780 students	624 students	

The Math Club's goal is to have 90% of the students in the school enter its contest.

How many more students need to enter the contest in order to meet the club's goal

_____

Show how you got your answer. Label your work so that it is clear.

Make a bar graph to show the percentages of students who were in the contest for the past three years. Compare the percents. What does your graph tell you?

Contest Rules

To enter the T-shirt design contest,
you must follow these rules.
Your design must

- be a tessellation that repeats at least
  three times.
- use at least two regular polygons.
- show at least two lines of symmetry.

In the box below, show your entry for this contest.
Make it actual size. Show that it fits within a 12-cm
square. Make a design your classmates would like.

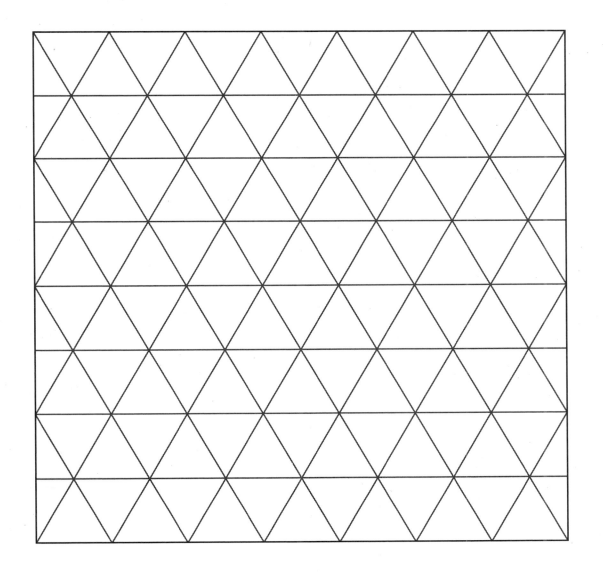

Name_____

Order the Color You Want

A T-shirt company at the beach is estimating how many T-shirts of each color to order. Last June, the T-shirt company sold the following numbers of shirts.

June T-Shirt Sales	
Color	Number Sold
Blue	500
White	800
Green	600
Black	100
Total	2,000

What percent of each color T-shirt was sold last June?
Make a circle graph to show the percent of each color sold.
Be sure to title and label your graph.

This June, the company expects the number of black T-shirt sales to triple. They want to keep the ratio of blue T-shirts to black T-shirts the same as it was last June.

What was the ratio last June? ——————

How many blue T-shirts will they need to order this year to

keep the ratio the same? _____

Show your work. Label your work so that how you got your ratios is clear.

Name

CHAPTERS 23-28

Cool T-Shirt Contest

Every year the Math Club has a contest to see who can design the best Cool T-Shirt. The following table shows the number of students who were in the contest for the past three years.

When?	Number of Students in School	Students Who Were in the Contest	Percent of Students in Contest
Two years ago	800 students	160 students	20%
Last year	850 students	340 students	40%
This year	780 students	624 students	80%

The Math Club's goal is to have 90% of the students in the school enter its contest.

How many more students need to enter the contest in order to meet the club's goal?

within 10%, or 78 students

Show how you got your answer. Label your work so that it is clear.

$780 \times 10\% = 78$ students
The Math Club needs 78 more students to sign up.

Make a bar graph to show the percentages of students who were in the contest for the past three years. Compare the percents. What does your graph tell you?
Explanations will vary.

Possible graph:

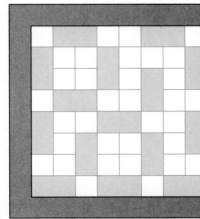

Math Club Contest

This Year / Last Year / Two Years Ago

650 600 550 500 450 400 350 300 250 200 150 100 50

T-Shirts D-2

60

Name

CHAPTERS 23-28

T-Shirts Logo

The Math Club is designing a new logo for its T-shirts. The design will have an 8 cm square with a 1 cm border around the square. An outline of the new logo is shown.

What is the area of the inside square?

$8 \text{ cm} \times 8 \text{ cm} = 64$ sq cm

What is the area of the outside square

$8 \text{ cm} + 2 \text{ cm} = 10 \text{ cm}$
$10 \text{ cm} \times 10 \text{ cm} = 100$ sq cm

The Math Club wants to use both 2-cm rectangles and 1-cm squares to form a design inside the frame. Draw a design of blocks that will fit inside the frame. How many squares and rectangles will fit inside the frame?

Possible answer:

Show and label your work.
Possible answer: 34 1-cm squares and 15 2-cm rectangles

T-Shirts D-1

59

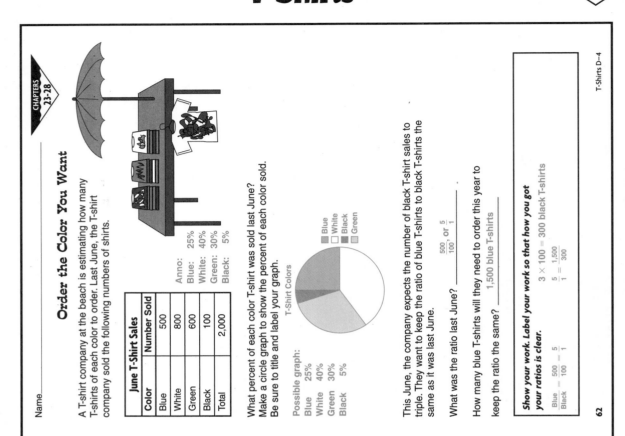

Name _____

CHAPTERS
23-28

Order the Color You Want

A T-shirt company at the beach is estimating how many T-shirts of each color to order. Last June, the T-shirt company sold the following numbers of shirts.

June T-Shirt Sales

Color	Number Sold
Blue	500
White	800
Green	600
Black	100
Total	2,000

Anno:
Blue: 25%
White: 40%
Green: 30%
Black: 5%

What percent of each color T-shirt was sold last June?
Make a circle graph to show the percent of each color sold.
Be sure to title and label your graph.

T-Shirt Colors

Possible graph:
Blue 25%
White 40%
Green 30%
Black 5%

■ Blue
□ White
■ Black
■ Green

This June, the company expects the number of black T-shirt sales to triple. They want to keep the ratio of blue T-shirts to black T-shirts the same as it was last June.

What was the ratio last June? ___ $\frac{500}{100}$, or $\frac{5}{1}$

How many blue T-shirts will they need to order this year to keep the ratio the same? ___ 1,500 blue T-shirts

Show your work. Label your work so that how you got your ratios is clear.

3 × 100 = 300 black T-shirts

Blue = $\frac{500}{100} = \frac{5}{1}$ $\frac{5}{1} = \frac{1,500}{300}$
Black

62

T-Shirts D–4

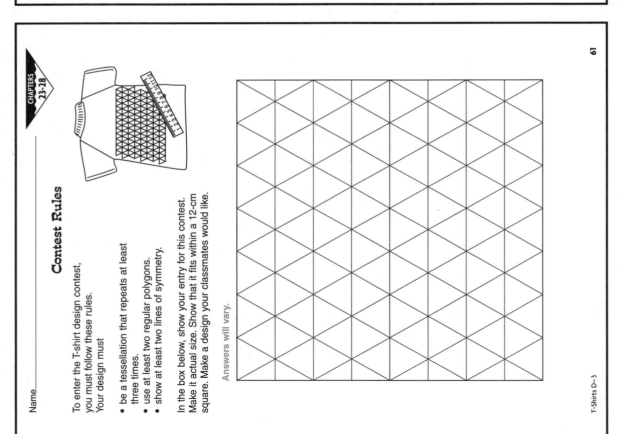

Name _____

CHAPTERS
23-28

Contest Rules

To enter the T-shirt design contest, you must follow these rules.
Your design must

• be a tessellation that repeats at least three times.
• use at least two regular polygons.
• show at least two lines of symmetry.

In the box below, show your entry for this contest. Make it actual size. Show that it fits within a 12-cm square. Make a design your classmates would like.

Answers will vary.

T-Shirts D–3

61

T-Shirts

Left Panel (Level 3)

Name _____

T-Shirts Logo

The Math Club is designing a new logo for its T-shirts. The design will have an 8-cm square with a 1-cm border around the square. An outline of the new logo is shown.

What is the area of the inside square?
64 sq. cm

What is the area of the outside square
100 sq. cm

The Math Club wants to use both 2-cm rectangles and 1-cm squares to form a pattern inside the frame. Draw a pattern of blocks that will fit inside the frame. How many squares and rectangles will fit inside the frame?

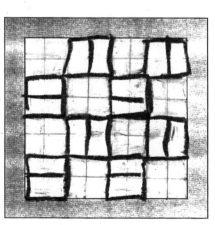

Show and label your work.
64 sq. in 32 rectangles 2cm   64 ÷ 2 = 32
↓ 8×8=64   →8 length ×8 width=64 area   } because 2cm×cm×kcm

Level 3 The student successfully completed all or most parts of the task. The intents of all parts of the task were addressed with an understanding of appropriate strategies and procedures. The student's work and explanations are clear and easy to follow but did not show or explain how the student got 100 sq cm. Answers for all parts are correct.

Right Panel (Level 2)

Name _____

T-Shirts Logo

The Math Club is designing a new logo for its T-shirts. The design will have an 8-cm square with a 1-cm border around the square. An outline of the new logo is shown.

What is the area of the inside square?
64 sq. cm

What is the area of the outside square
100 sq cm

The Math Club wants to use both 2-cm rectangles and 1-cm squares to form a pattern inside the frame. Draw a pattern of blocks that will fit inside the frame. How many squares and rectangles will fit inside the frame?

32 squares
16 rectangles

64
36
100

Show and label your work. first we divided off the box into to segments the center 64 for the inside. Then we found out anser for the side is 36. then we added 64 and 36 and we got 100.

Level 2 The student successfully completed some of the parts. There is evidence that the student has partial understanding of concepts and procedures. Some explanations are clear, but you may need to make inferences to understand the responses. Answers are correct for some parts, but explanations are incomplete for others.

Model Student Papers for
T-Shirts

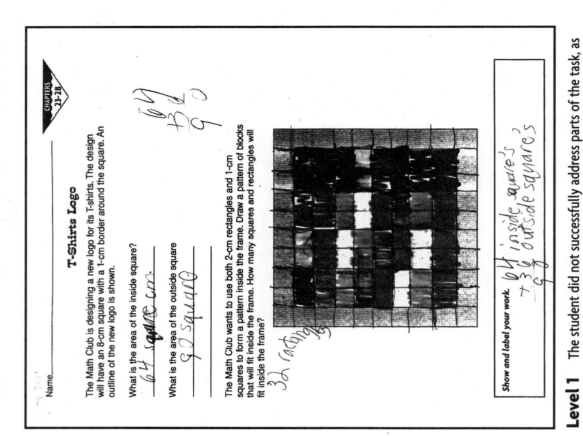

Name _____

T-Shirts Logo

The Math Club is designing a new logo for its T-shirts. The design will have an 8-cm square with a 1-cm border around the square. An outline of the new logo is shown.

What is the area of the inside square?
64 square cm.

What is the area of the outside square
80 square

The Math Club wants to use both 2-cm rectangles and 1-cm squares to form a pattern inside the frame. Draw a pattern of blocks that will fit inside the frame. How many squares and rectangles will fit inside the frame?

32 rectangles

Show and label your work.
64 inside squares
+36 outside squares
—————
67

Level 1 The student did not successfully address parts of the task, as in the explanation of steps. There is minimal or limited evidence that the student understands concepts and procedures. The student's work is difficult to follow and requires you to fill in gaps. The student offered no explanations for the work. Answers for most parts are incorrect.

TEACHER NOTES

Level 3 paper

Name _____

CHAPTERS 23-28

Cool T-Shirt Contest

Every year the Math Club has a contest to see who can design the best Cool T-Shirt. The following table shows the number of students who were in the contest for the past three years.

When?	Number of Students in School	Students Who Were in the Contest	Percent of Students in Contest
Two years ago	800 students	160 students	20%
Last year	850 students	340 students	40%
This year	780 students	624 students	80%

The Math Club's goal is to have 90% of the students in the school enter its contest.

How close is the club to reaching its goal? They are 10% away

Show how you got your answer. Label your work so that it is clear.

two years ago   Last year   This year
160 ÷ 800 = .2 = 20%   340 ÷ 850 = 2.5 = 40%   624 ÷ 780 = .8 = 80%

80% is 10% away from 90%.

Make a bar graph to show the percentages of students who were in the contest for the past three years. Compare the percents. What does your graph tell you?

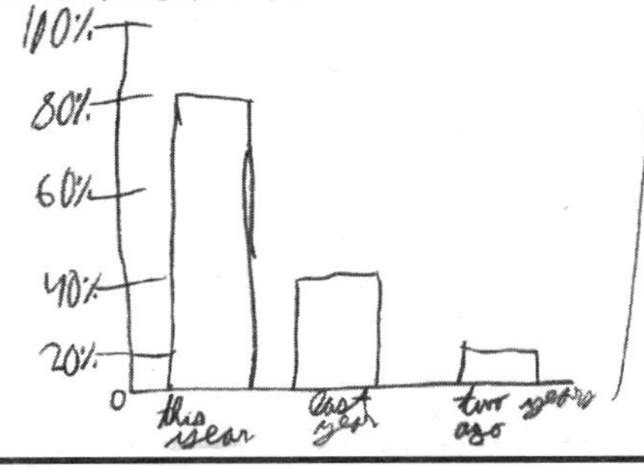

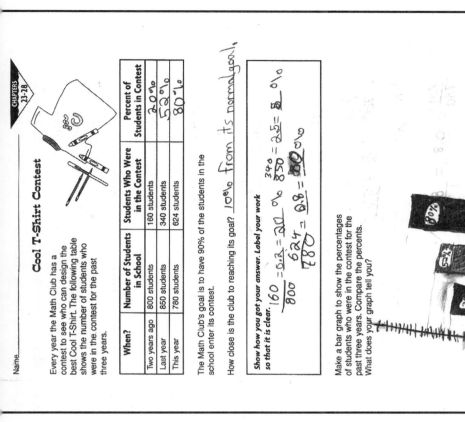

This graph shows that participation is climbing each year.

60   T-Shirts D-2

Level 3 The student successfully completed all or most parts of the task. The intents of all parts of the task were addressed with an understanding of appropriate strategies and procedures. The student's work and explanations are clear and easy to follow. Answers for all parts are correct.

Level 2 paper

Name _____

CHAPTERS 23-28

Cool T-Shirt Contest

Every year the Math Club has a contest to see who can design the best Cool T-Shirt. The following table shows the number of students who were in the contest for the past three years.

When?	Number of Students in School	Students Who Were in the Contest	Percent of Students in Contest
Two years ago	800 students	160 students	20%
Last year	850 students	340 students	52%
This year	780 students	624 students	80%

The Math Club's goal is to have 90% of the students in the school enter its contest.

How close is the club to reaching its goal? 10% from its normal goal.

Show how you got your answer. Label your work so that it is clear.

160 = 62 = 20%   340 = 25 = 52%
800   850

624 ÷ 0.8 = 80%
780

Make a bar graph to show the percentages of students who were in the contest for the past three years. Compare the percents. What does your graph tell you?

Two yrs ago   Last yr   This year

60   T-Shirts D-2

Level 2 The student successfully completed some of the parts; other parts were not successfully completed. There is evidence that the student has partial understanding of concepts. Some explanations are clear, but you may need to make inferences to understand the responses. Answers are correct for some parts but are partially correct or incorrect for others.

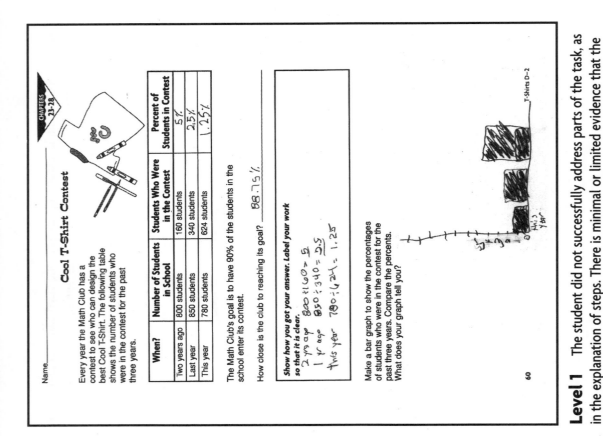

CHAPTERS 23-28

Cool T-Shirt Contest

Name _____

Every year the Math Club has a contest to see who can design the best Cool T-Shirt. The following table shows the number of students who were in the contest for the past three years.

When?	Number of Students in School	Students Who Were in the Contest	Percent of Students in Contest
Two years ago	800 students	160 students	5%
Last year	850 students	340 students	25%
This year	780 students	624 students	1.25%

The Math Club's goal is to have 90% of the students in the school enter its contest.

How close is the club to reaching its goal? 88.75%

Show how you got your answer. Label your work so that it is clear.

2 yrs ago   800 ÷ 160 = 5
1 yr ago   850 ÷ 340 = 0.5
this year   780 ÷ 624 = 1.25

Make a bar graph to show the percentages of students who were in the contest for the past three years. Compare the percents. What does your graph tell you?

60

T-Shirts D-2

TEACHER NOTES

Level 1   The student did not successfully address parts of the task, as in the explanation of steps. There is minimal or limited evidence that the student understands concepts and procedures. The student's work is difficult to follow and requires you to fill in gaps. The student offered no explanations for the work. Answers for most parts are incorrect.

Model Student Papers for
T-Shirts

Name _____

Contest Rules

To enter the T-shirt design contest,
you must follow these rules.
Your design must

- be a tessellation that repeats at least
  three times.
- use at least two regular polygons.
- show at least two lines of symmetry.

In the box below, show your entry for this contest.
Make it actual size. Show that it fits within a 12-cm
square. Make a design your classmates would like.

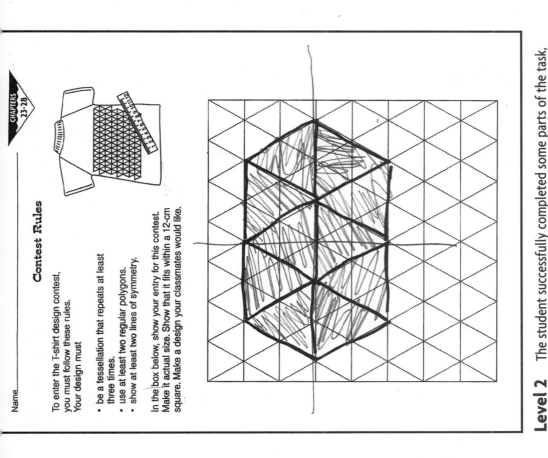

Level 2 The student successfully completed some parts of the task,
and there is evidence the student has a partial understanding of the procedures. Instead of using two regular polygons, the student drew a tessellation using one equilateral triangle. Two lines of symmetry are shown.

Name _____

Contest Rules

To enter the T-shirt design contest,
you must follow these rules.
Your design must

- be a tessellation that repeats at least
  three times.
- use at least two regular polygons.
- show at least two lines of symmetry.

In the box below, show your entry for this contest.
Make it actual size. Show that it fits within a 12-cm
square. Make a design your classmates would like.

Level 3 The student successfully completes all of the task with
appropriate strategies and procedures. The student has a clear understanding of key concepts and procedures. The student's work is clear. A tessellation using a regular hexagon and equilateral triangle is shown, along with
two lines of symmetry.

Model Student Papers for
T-Shirts

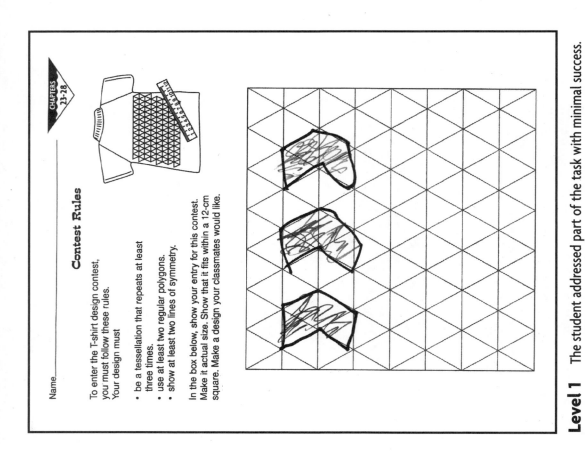

Name _____

Contest Rules

To enter the T-shirt design contest, you must follow these rules. Your design must

- be a tessellation that repeats at least three times.
- use at least two regular polygons.
- show at least two lines of symmetry.

In the box below, show your entry for this contest. Make it actual size. Show that it fits within a 12-cm square. Make a design your classmates would like.

Level 1 The student addressed part of the task with minimal success. There is limited evidence that the student understands key concepts or procedures. The student drew a pattern that is not a tessellation, using a figure that is not a regular polygon. No lines of symmetry are drawn.

TEACHER NOTES

Level 3

CHAPTERS 23-28

Name: _____

Order the Color You Want

A T-shirt company at the beach is estimating how many T-shirts of each color to order. Last June, the T-shirt company sold the following numbers of shirts.

June T-Shirt Sales

Color	Number Sold
Blue	500
White	800
Green	600
Black	100
Total	2,000

What percent of each color T-shirt was sold last June? Make a circle graph to show the percent of each color sold. Be sure to title and label your graph.

This June, the company expects the number of black T-shirt sales to triple. They want to keep the ratio of blue T-shirts to black T-shirts the same as it was last June.

What was the ratio last June? $\dfrac{500}{100}$

How many blue T-shirts will they need to order this year to keep the ratio the same? 1,500

Show your work. Label your work so that how you got your ratios is clear.

blue - $\frac{500}{2000}$ = 25%   black $\frac{100}{2000}$ = 5%
white - $\frac{800}{2000}$ = 40%
green - $\frac{600}{2000}$ = 30%

Level 3 The student successfully completed all or most parts of the task. The intents of all parts of the task were addressed with an understanding of appropriate strategies and procedures. The student's work is clear and easy to follow. Answers for all parts are correct.

Level 2

CHAPTERS 23-28

Name: _____

Order the Color You Want

A T-shirt company at the beach is estimating how many T-shirts of each color to order. Last June, the T-shirt company sold the following numbers of shirts.

June T-Shirt Sales

Color	Number Sold
Blue	500
White	800
Green	600
Black	100
Total	2,000

What percent of each color T-shirt was sold last June? Make a circle graph to show the percent of each color sold. Be sure to title and label your graph.

This June, the company expects the number of black T-shirt sales to triple. They want to keep the ratio of blue T-shirts to black T-shirts the same as it was last June.

What was the ratio last June? $\dfrac{500}{100}$

How many blue T-shirts will they need to order this year to keep the ratio the same? 1500

Show your work. Label your work so that how you got your ratios is clear.

$\dfrac{500 \times 3 = 1500}{100 \times 3 = 300}$

Level 2 The student successfully completed some of the parts; other parts were not successfully completed. There is evidence that the student has partial understanding of concepts. Lack of explanations leads you to make inferences to understand the responses. Answers for some parts are correct but answers are partially correct or incorrect for others.

Model Student Papers for
T-Shirts

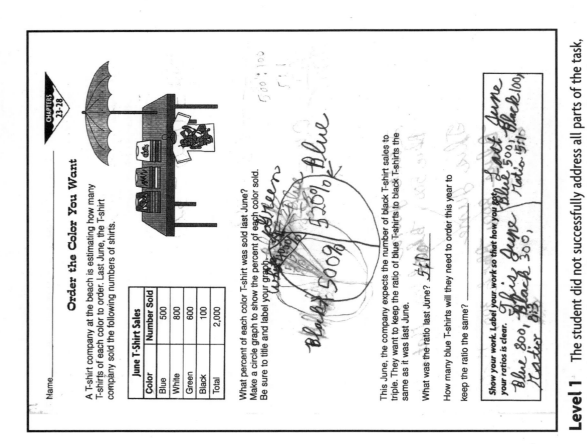

Name _____

Order the Color You Want

A T-shirt company at the beach is estimating how many T-shirts of each color to order. Last June, the T-shirt company sold the following numbers of shirts.

June T-Shirt Sales	
Color	Number Sold
Blue	500
White	800
Green	600
Black	100
Total	2,000

What percent of each color T-shirt was sold last June?
Make a circle graph to show the percent of each color sold.
Be sure to title and label your graph.

This June, the company expects the number of black T-shirt sales to triple. They want to keep the ratio of blue T-shirts to black T-shirts the same as it was last June.

What was the ratio last June? _5700_

How many blue T-shirts will they need to order this year to keep the ratio the same? _____

Show your work. Label your work so that how you got your ratios is clear.

TEACHER NOTES

Level 1 The student did not successfully address all parts of the task, as in the explanation of steps. There is minimal or limited evidence that the student understands concepts and procedures. The student's work is difficult to follow and requires you to fill in gaps. The student offers few explanations for the work. Answers for most parts are incorrect.

Performance Assessment

Class Record Form

School	Assessment A					Assessment B				
	Task A-1	Task A-2	Task A-3	Task A-4	Total	Task B-1	Task B-2	Task B-3	Task B-4	Total
Teacher										
NAMES Date										

Performance Assessment

Class Record Form

School	Assessment C					Assessment D				
	Task C-1	Task C-2	Task C-3	Task C-4	Total	Task D-1	Task D-2	Task D-3	Task D-4	Total
Teacher										
NAMES Date										

Evaluating Interview/Task Test Items

The interview/task test items are designed to provide an optional instrument to evaluate each child's level of accomplishment for each learning goal of the *Math Advantage* program. These items provide opportunities for children to verbalize or write about his or her thinking or to use manipulatives or other pictorial representations to represent their thinking. They test children at the concrete and pictorial levels, where appropriate, so that you can assess each child's progress toward functioning at the abstract level. The items will enable you to analyze the child's thought processes as they work on different types of problems and will enable you to plan instruction that will meet your children's needs.

You may wish to use these test items as you work through the content in the chapter to determine whether children are ready to move on or whether they need additional teaching or reinforcement activities. You may also wish to use these test items with children who did not successfully pass the chapter test to determine what types of reteaching activities are appropriate. These test items may also be used with students who have difficulty reading written material or who have learning disabilities.

The test items are designed to focus on evaluating how children think about mathematics and how they work at solving problems rather than on whether they can get the correct answer. The evaluation criteria given for each test item will help you pinpoint the errors in the children's thinking processes as they work through the problem.

A checklist of possible responses is provided to record each child's thinking processes. The Class Record Form can be used to show satisfactory comple-tion of interview/task test items.

Evaluation of Interview/Task Test

Date _____

Student's Name _____

Materials: place-value chart on PE page 6, counters

TEST ITEM	EVALUATE WHETHER STUDENT
1-A.1 *To identify a number as ordinal, nominal, or cardinal* Give a number for each. Then explain how you know whether the number is expressed as cardinal, ordinal, or nominal. • your phone number • the number of letters in your name • the position in the alphabet of the letter *E*	_____ names a number for each correctly. _____ explains that the phone number names something and is a nominal number. _____ explains that the number of letters in a name tells how many and is a cardinal number. _____ explains that the position of *E* in the alphabet tells order and is an ordinal number.
1-A.2 *To use a benchmark number to estimate quantity* Put 10 counters in a group. Then take a handful of counters and put them in a second group. Explain how you can use the group of 10 counters as a benchmark to estimate the number of counters in the second group. Estimate the number of counters in the second group.	_____ explains how the second group of counters can be compared to the group of 10 counters. _____ gives a reasonable estimate for the number of counters in the handful.
1-A.3 *To identify place value and read and identify numbers to millions* Write a 6-digit number. Look at the place-value chart on page 6. Make a place-value chart for your number. Use your chart to explain the value of each digit. Then read your number.	_____ writes a 6-digit number. _____ writes the number correctly in a place-value chart. _____ explains the value of each digit in the number. _____ reads the number correctly.
1-A.4 *To compare and order numbers to millions* Explain how to use place value to order these numbers from least to greatest: 5,608; 5,860; 5,806. Then write the numbers in order.	_____ explains that to order numbers you compare the digits in each place-value position starting at the left. _____ explains that the numbers have the same number of thousands. _____ explains that since 6 hundreds is less than 8 hundreds, 5,608 is the least number. _____ explains that since 0 tens is less than 6 tens, 5,806 is the next number. _____ identifies the order of the numbers as 5,608; 5,806; 5,860.

TEST ITEM	EVALUATE WHETHER STUDENT

2-A.1 *To use addition and subtraction as inverse operations*
 	
Solve each problem. Explain how you can use the inverse operation to check your answer. Check each problem.
 	
    58   75
    + 31   − 62
	_____ identifies 89 as the solution to the first problem.
	
	_____ identifies 13 as the solution to the second problem.
	
	_____ explains that addition and subtraction are inverse operations, which means that one operation undoes the other operation.
	
	_____ uses subtraction to check the first problem. $\begin{array}{r} 89 \\ -\,31 \end{array}$
	
	_____ uses addition to check the second problem. $\begin{array}{r} 13 \\ +\,62 \end{array}$

2-A.2 *To subtract across zeros with regrouping* Show and explain each step as you find the difference. $\begin{array}{r} 6{,}080 \\ -\,1{,}245 \end{array}$	_____ explains that you have to regroup to subtract ones and regroups correctly. _____ explains that you have to regroup to subtract hundreds and regroups correctly. _____ identifies the difference as 4,835.
2-A.3 *To choose the operation to solve problems* Tell whether you would add or subtract to solve each problem. Then explain your choice and solve the problem. *Erica has 372 stamps in her collection. Anna has 556 stamps in her collection. How many more stamps does Anna have?* *Jon collected 285 shells at the beach last year and 97 shells this year. How many shells did he collect in the two years?*	for the first problem: _____ chooses subtraction to solve the problem. _____ explains that you subtract to compare numbers. _____ identifies the solution as 184 stamps. for the second problem: _____ chooses addition to solve the problem. _____ explains that you add to join groups. _____ identifies the solution as 382 shells.

2-A.4 *To estimate sums and differences*
 	
Explain the method you would use to estimate this sum. Then give the estimate.   319
          592
          107
     + 680
	_____ rounds the numbers to the nearest hundred: 300, 600, 100, 700. (Answers may vary if rounded to the nearest ten.)
	
	_____ adds the rounded numbers.
	
	_____ identifies the estimated sum as 1,700.

Student's Name_____

Materials: base-ten blocks, place-value chart on PE page 40, number line on PE page 44

TEST ITEM	EVALUATE WHETHER STUDENT
3-A.1 *To read and write decimals in tenths and hundredths* Use base-ten blocks to model the number two and fifteen hundredths. Draw a picture of your model. Then write the number and explain the value of each digit.	_____ shows a correct model for the number. _____ draws a picture for the model. _____ writes the number as 2.15. _____ explains the value of each digit: 2 ones, 1 tenth, 5 hundredths.
3-A.2 *To read and write numbers from thousands to thousandths in standard and expanded form* Look at the place-value chart on page 40. Make a place-value chart for 1,234.567. Use your chart to explain the value of each digit. Then read the number and write it in expanded form.	_____ shows the number correctly in a place-value chart. _____ explains the value of each digit: 1 thousand, 2 hundreds, 3 tens, 4 ones, 5 tenths, 6 hundredths, 7 thousandths. _____ reads the number correctly. _____ writes the number in expanded form: $1000 + 200 + 30 + 4 + 0.5 + 0.06 + 0.007$.
3-A.3 *To identify and write equivalent decimals* Write an equivalent decimal for each. Explain how you know the decimals are equivalent. 0.5 0.360 1.22	_____ writes an equivalent decimal for each. (Possible answers: 0.50, 0.36, 1.220) _____ explains why the decimals are equivalent. (Possible explanation: The base-ten block model would be the same size for equivalent decimals.)
3-A.4 *To compare and order decimals* Explain how to order these numbers from least to greatest by using either the number line on page 44 or by comparing the digits in the numbers. 8.75 8.36 8.49	_____ explains how to order the numbers by looking at the positions of the numbers on the number line or by comparing the digits beginning at the left. _____ identifies the order as 8.36, 8.49, 8.75.

TEST ITEM	EVALUATE WHETHER STUDENT
4-A.1 *To add and subtract decimals* Show and explain each step as you solve these problems. $2.51 + 6.208 = n$ $8.5 - 3.19 = n$	for the first problem: _____ aligns the numbers correctly to add. _____ regroups and adds correctly. _____ identifies the sum as 8.718. for the second problem: _____ aligns the numbers correctly to subtract. _____ regroups and subtracts correctly. _____ identifies the difference as 5.31.
4-A.2 *To estimate decimal sums and differences* Show and explain each step as you estimate the sum or difference by rounding to the nearest hundredth. $\begin{array}{r} 2.149 \\ + 4.352 \end{array}$ $\begin{array}{r} 5.587 \\ - 1.204 \end{array}$	for the first problem: _____ rounds the numbers correctly: 2.149 rounds to 2.15 and 4.352 rounds to 4.35. _____ adds the rounded numbers. _____ identifies the estimated sum as 6.50. for the second problem: _____ rounds the numbers correctly: 5.587 rounds to 5.59 and 1.204 rounds to 1.20. _____ subtracts the rounded numbers. _____ identifies the estimated difference as 4.39.
4-A.3 *To solve problems by choosing the operation and writing a number sentence* Tell whether you would add or subtract to solve each problem. Then explain your choice and solve the problem. *Anthony spent $4.39 for groceries and $2.56 for school supplies. How much did he spend in all?* *Jennifer had a $5 bill. She bought a book for $3.79. How much change did she receive?*	for the first problem: _____ chooses addition to solve the problem. _____ explains that you add to join groups. _____ identifies the solution as $6.95. for the second problem: _____ chooses subtraction to solve the problem. _____ explains that you subtract to take away part of the group. _____ identifies the solution as $1.21.

Evaluation of Interview/Task Test

Date _____

Student's Name _____

TEST ITEM	EVALUATE WHETHER STUDENT
5-A.1 *To identify and use multiplication properties* Explain the property of multiplication you would use to complete each equation. Then give the missing number. $7 \times \square = 0$ $3 \times 5 = \square \times 3$ $1 \times 9 = \square$ $(3 \times 1) \times 8 = 3 \times (\square \times 8)$	explains how the properties apply to these facts: _____ $7 \times \square = 0 \rightarrow$ explains that the Property of Zero states that if one factor is zero, the product is zero. _____ $3 \times 5 = \square \times 3 \rightarrow$ explains that the Commutative Property states that you can multiply numbers in any order; the product is the same. _____ $1 \times 9 = \square \rightarrow$ explains that the Property of One states that when one of the factor is 1, the product equals the other number. _____ $(3 \times 1) \times 8 = 3 \times (\square \times 8) \rightarrow$ explains that the Associative Property states that you can group factors differently; the product is always the same. identifies the missing numbers in the equations as: _____ $7 \times \mathbf{0} = 0$; _____ $3 \times 5 = \mathbf{5} \times 3$; _____ $1 \times 9 = \mathbf{9}$; _____ $(3 \times 1) \times 8 = 3 \times (\mathbf{1} \times 8)$
5-A.2 *To multiply by one-digit numbers* Show and explain each step as you find the product of 6×418.	_____ multiplies and regroups correctly. _____ aligns the partial products correctly. _____ identifies the product as 2,508.
5-A.3 *To use formulas to find area and volume* Show and explain each step as you use a formula to find • the area of a rug that is 4 ft by 12 ft. • the volume of a box that is 5 in. $\times$ 4 in. $\times$ 2 in.	_____ explains how to use the formula for area, $A = l \times w$. _____ identifies the area as 48 sq ft. _____ explains how to use the formula for volume, $V = l \times w \times h$, to find the volume of the box. _____ identifies the volume as 40 cubic in.

TEST ITEM	EVALUATE WHETHER STUDENT
6-A.1 *To multiply by two- or three-digit numbers* Show and explain each step as you find the product of 526 × 371.	_____ multiplies and regroups correctly. _____ aligns the partial products correctly. _____ identifies the product as 195,146.
6-A.2 *To estimate products* Estimate the product of 68 × 23 by rounding factors to the nearest ten. Show and explain your method.	_____ rounds the factors to the nearest ten: 68 rounds to 70; 23 rounds to 20. _____ uses basic facts to name the estimated product. _____ identifies the estimated product as 1,400.
6-A.3 *To multiply to find perimeter and area* Show and explain each step as you find the perimeter and the area of a sandbox that is 8 feet by 10 feet.	_____ explains that perimeter is distance around a figure and that to find the perimeter of a rectangle you multiply the length and width by 2 and add the products. _____ identifies the perimeter as 36 ft. _____ explains that you multiply the length by the width to find the area, $A = l \times w$. _____ identifies the area as 80 sq ft.

Evaluation of Interview/Task Test

Date _____

Student's Name_____

TEST ITEM	EVALUATE WHETHER STUDENT
7-A.1 *To estimate a quotient* Describe compatible numbers. Then explain each step as you use compatible numbers to estimate the quotient of 216 ÷ 7.	_____ explains that compatible numbers are numbers close to the actual numbers that can be divided evenly. _____ chooses appropriate compatible numbers (such as 210 ÷ 7). _____ uses mental math to estimate. _____ identifies an appropriate estimated quotient (such as 30).
7-A.2 *To divide by one-digit numbers* Show and explain each step as you find the quotient of 812 ÷ 4.	_____ estimates the quotient as about 200. _____ aligns the numbers correctly while computing. _____ writes 0 in the tens place in the quotient. _____ computes correctly. _____ identifies the quotient as 203.
7-A.3 *To solve problems using the **guess-and-check** strategy* Explain how you could use the *guess-and-check* strategy to solve this problem. Then solve the problem. *Laurie has 131 photos. She puts an equal number of photos on each page in an album and then has 5 photos left over. How many pages have photos on them? How many photos are on each page?*	_____ explains how to guess an answer and then check to see if the guess is correct. _____ identifies a correct solution. (One possible solution: 14 pages with 9 photos on each page.)

TEST ITEM	EVALUATE WHETHER STUDENT
8-A.1 *To use patterns of zeros and estimation to divide* Explain how you can use mental math and patterns of zeros to find the quotient of $6,000 \div 20$.	_____ explains that the quotient has two zeros. _____ identifies the quotient as 300.
8-A.2 *To estimate quotients* Show and explain each step as you use compatible numbers to estimate the quotient of $4,215 \div 58$.	_____ chooses appropriate compatible numbers (such as $4,200 \div 60$). _____ uses mental math to estimate. _____ identifies an appropriate estimated quotient (such as 70).
8-A.3 *To divide by two-digit numbers* Show and explain each step as you find the quotient of $3,580 \div 42$.	_____ estimates to place the first digit in the quotient. _____ aligns the numbers correctly while computing. _____ computes correctly. _____ records the remainder correctly. _____ identifies the quotient as 85 r10.
8-A.4 *To solve problems by choosing the operation and writing a number sentence* Tell whether you would add, subtract, multiply, or divide to solve this problem. Then explain your choice, and write a number sentence to solve the problem. *Anthony has $1,800 in his bank account. He has been depositing $75 in the account each month. For how many months has he been making deposits?* *Jolyn deposited $15 in her bank account each month for 36 months. How much money did Jolyn deposit in the account?*	for the first problem: _____ chooses division to solve the problem. _____ explains that you divide to find how much or how many are in each group. _____ identifies the solution as 24 months. for the second problem: _____ chooses multiplication to solve the problem. _____ explains that you multiply to combine equal-size groups. _____ identifies the solution as $540.

Evaluation of Interview/Task Test

Date _____

Student's Name _____

Materials: connecting cubes, table on PE page 156

TEST ITEM	EVALUATE WHETHER STUDENT
9-A.1 *To compute the mean of a set of data* Use connecting cubes to help you find the mean for this set of data: 3, 8, 4, 5, 5. Explain each step.	_____ uses cubes to model each number in the set of data. _____ explains that to find the mean, you move cubes so that the five stacks of cubes are equal. _____ identifies the mean as 5.
9-A.2 *To choose a reasonable scale for a set of data* Look at the data on the number of tickets sold each day in the table at the top of page 156. What scale would you use to make a line graph of this data? Explain your choice.	_____ chooses a reasonable scale, such as 0, 2, 4, 6, 8, 10. _____ explains that the scale is reasonable because it would be easy to read the data on a graph with this scale.
9-A.3 *To make and use line graphs* Explain each step as you make a line graph for this data. **Inches of Rainfall** Month Apr May Jun Jul Inches 4 3 5 7	_____ chooses an appropriate scale. _____ labels the graph with the months and the inches. _____ shows the data on the graph. _____ joins the data with a line. _____ writes a title for the graph.
9-A.4 *To choose the appropriate graph to display data* Choose a type of graph or plot you would use to display the data. Explain your choice. • the number of students in the fifth-grade classes at school. • the scores on a fifth-grade spelling test. • the outdoor temperature at noon for one week.	chooses an appropriate graph or plot, such as _____ number of students in fifth-grade classes → bar graph to compare the data. _____ scores on a spelling test → stem-and-leaf plot to organize data by place value. _____ outdoor temperature → line graph to show change over time.

aterials: circle graph on PE page 176, teacher-made bar graph, sample graphs (circle, line, bar)

TEST ITEM	EVALUATE WHETHER STUDENT
10-A.1 *To read and interpret circle graphs* Look at the circle graph on page 176 showing the 10 items in Jenna's desk. Explain how the circle graph would change if Jenna had 4 pencils, 4 notebooks, and 2 erasers in her desk. Then explain what the whole circle represents.	_____ explains that 4 sections of the graph would be labeled Pencils, 4 sections would be labeled Notebooks, and the sections labeled Erasers would stay the same. _____ explains that the whole circle represents all 10 items in Jenna's desk.
10-A.2 *To determine if data is accurately shown in a graph* Beth's Trophy Collection Soccer 4 Trophies Softball 2 Trophies Basketball 1 Trophy Swimming 3 Trophies Explain why the graph is not accurate and how you would change the graph to make it accurate.	_____ explains that the bar for Swimming is the wrong height. _____ explains that the bar for Swimming should be drawn to show 3 trophies.
10-A.3 *To compare data displayed in different kinds of graphs* Identify the type of graph you would choose to display data for each situation: • to keep track of the attendance in your classroom for one month. • to show how you spent a $5 birthday gift. • to compare the heights of ten friends. Explain your choices.	chooses an appropriate graph, such as _____ attendance in classroom → line graph to show change over time. _____ how you spent $5 → circle graph to compare parts of a group to the whole group. _____ heights of ten friends → bar graph to compare data.

Evaluation of Interview/Task Test

Date _____

Student's Name_____

Materials: optional (spinner with 6 parts; bag with 3 red marbles, 2 blue marbles, and 1 yellow marble)

TEST ITEM	EVALUATE WHETHER STUDENT
11-A.1 *To determine if events are certain, impossible, likely, or unlikely* Suppose you have a spinner that is numbered 1, 2, 3, 5, 7, 9. Describe each event as certain, impossible, likely, or unlikely. Explain your choices. • spinning an odd number. • spinning an even number. • spinning a number less than 10. • spinning the number 12.	_____ describes spinning an odd number as likely because 5 of the 6 numbers are odd. _____ describes spinning an even number as unlikely because only 1 of the 6 numbers is even. _____ describes spinning a number less than 10 as certain because all the numbers are less than 10. _____ describes spinning the number 12 as impossible because the number is not on the spinner.
11-A.2 *To make a tree diagram and solve problems by making a list* Explain each step as you make a tree diagram to show the number of different color combinations Megan has if she can choose from blue, brown, and green shorts and from white, yellow, red, and black tops.	_____ draws a tree diagram correctly to show 3 possible colors for shorts with 4 possible colors for tops for each pair of shorts. _____ explains that the tree diagram shows that there are 12 different color combinations possible.
11-A.3 *To find the probability of an event and compare probabilities of separate events* Suppose there are 3 red marbles, 2 blue marbles, and 1 yellow marble in a bag. Describe the probability of pulling • a red marble. • a blue marble. • a yellow marble. • a black marble. Explain how you determined the probabilities. Then explain whether it is more likely that you will pull a yellow marble or a red marble from the bag.	_____ describes the probabilities as: red: $\frac{3}{6}$, or $\frac{1}{2}$; blue: $\frac{2}{6}$, or $\frac{1}{3}$; yellow: $\frac{1}{6}$; black: $\frac{0}{6}$, or 0. _____ explains that a fraction (showing the number of ways the event can occur over the number of ways all events can occur) can be used to describe probability. _____ explains that it is more likely you will pull a red marble than a yellow marble because $\frac{1}{2} > \frac{1}{6}$.

udent's Name_____

aterials: 10 x 10 grid, colored pencils or markers

TEST ITEM	EVALUATE WHETHER STUDENT
12-A.1 *To identify and use patterns in decimal factors and products* Explain the pattern you see in these problems. Then explain how to use mental math to find and name the products. $45 \times 1 = n$ $45 \times 0.1 = n$ $45 \times 0.01 = n$	_____ explains that the decimal point moves one place to the left in the second factor in each problem. _____ explains that the decimal point will also move one place to the left in the products. _____ identifies the products as 45, 4.5, and 0.45.
12-A.2 *To multiply decimals by whole numbers and decimals by decimals* Use a 10 by 10 grid and colored pencils or markers to show the product of 0.4×0.6. Describe the part of the grid that shows the product.	_____ shades 4 of the ten rows one color. _____ shades 6 of the 10 columns another color. _____ explains that the squares shaded by both colors represent the product. _____ identifies the product as 0.24.
12-A.3 *To use estimation to place the decimal point in the product* Explain how you would estimate to place the decimal point in each product. Then find the product. $\begin{array}{cc} 5.2 & 0.22 \\ \times\ 12 & \times\ 0.06 \end{array}$	for the first problem: _____ explains an appropriate way to estimate, such as *rounding* 5.2 to $5.0 \times 12 = 60$; so, the product is about 60. _____ identifies the product as 62.4. for the second problem: _____ explains an appropriate way to estimate, such as *looking for patterns:* there are 2 decimal places in each factor; so, there will be 4 decimal places in the product. _____ identifies the product as 0.0132.
12-A.4 *To multiply mixed decimals* Show and explain each step as you find the product of 2.4×0.61.	_____ estimates the product as about 2. _____ computes correctly. _____ aligns the partial products correctly. _____ places the decimal point in the product correctly. _____ identifies the product as 1.464.

Evaluation of Interview/Task Test

Student's Name _____

Date _____

TEST ITEM	EVALUATE WHETHER STUDENT
13-A.1 *To identify patterns when dividing multiples of ten* Explain the pattern you see in these problems. Then explain how to use mental math to find the quotients and name the quotients. $300 \div 6 = n$ $30 \div 6 = n$ $3 \div 6 = n$	_____ explains that there is one less zero in the dividend in each problem. _____ explains that the decimal point will move one place to the left in the quotients. _____ identifies the quotients as 50, 5, and 0.5.
13-A.2 *To divide decimals by whole numbers and use patterns or estimation to place the decimal point* Show and explain each step as you use patterns or estimation to place the decimal point, and then find the quotient. $8)\overline{32.8}$	_____ estimates the quotient. _____ aligns the numbers correctly while computing. _____ places the decimal point correctly in the quotient. _____ identifies the quotient as 4.1.
13-A.3 *To choose the operation to solve problems* Tell whether you would multiply or divide to solve each problem. Then explain your choice and solve the problem. *Todd bought 7.5 pounds of apples and shared them equally with 2 friends. How many pounds of apples did each of the 3 people get?* *Theresa bought 5 packages of ground meat. There were 1.8 pounds of meat in each package. How many pounds of meat did she buy?*	for the first problem: _____ chooses division to solve the problem. _____ explains that you divide when you need to share something equally. _____ identifies the solution as 2.5 pounds. for the second problem: _____ chooses multiplication to solve the problem. _____ explains that you multiply when you need to join equal-size groups. _____ identifies the solution as 9 pounds.

Student's Name _____

Materials: metric tools for measuring length, capacity, and mass

TEST ITEM	EVALUATE WHETHER STUDENT
14-A.1 *To measure length in metric units* Which metric unit of length would you use to measure each object? Explain your choice. • length of a marker • distance from your home to the store • thickness of a button • length of your classroom	_____ chooses centimeters to measure the length of a marker. _____ chooses kilometers to measure the distance from home to the store. _____ chooses millimeters to measure the thickness of a button. _____ chooses meters to measure the length of the classroom. _____ explains the relative sizes of metric units of length.
14-A.2 *To use metric units to measure the mass of objects* Which metric unit of mass would you use to measure each object? Explain your choice. • a bag of potatoes • a stamp • a quarter	_____ chooses kilograms to measure the mass of a bag of potatoes. _____ chooses milligrams to measure the mass of a stamp. _____ chooses grams to measure the mass of a quarter. _____ uses the relative sizes of metric units of mass to explain choices.
14-A.3 *To identify the relationship between metric units* Explain how you know whether to multiply or divide when changing from one metric unit to another. Then explain how you know how to complete these statements. $3.7 \text{ cm} = \underline{\ ?\ } \text{ mm} \quad 45 \text{ g} = \underline{\ ?\ } \text{ mg}$ $3.7 \text{ cm} = \underline{\ ?\ } \text{ m} \quad 45 \text{ g} = \underline{\ ?\ } \text{ kg}$	_____ explains that you multiply to change units to smaller units and divide to change units to larger units. _____ identifies $3.7 \text{ cm} = 37 \text{ mm}$ and explains to multiply by 10 because millimeters are ten times smaller units than centimeters. _____ identifies $3.7 \text{ cm} = 0.037 \text{ m}$ and explains to divide by 100 because meters are 100 times larger units than centimeters. _____ identifies $45 \text{g} = 45{,}000 \text{ mg}$ and explains to multiply by 1,000 because milligrams are 1,000 times smaller units than grams. _____ identifies $45 \text{ g} = 0.045 \text{ kg}$ and explains to divide by 1,000 because kilograms are 1,000 times larger units than grams.

Evaluation of Interview/Task Test

Date _____

CHAPTER 15

Student's Name _____

Materials: fraction strip, number line, 4 squares each divided into fourths

TEST ITEM	EVALUATE WHETHER STUDENT
15-A.1 *To identify, read, and write fractions* Explain how you would use a fraction strip or a number line to show these fractions. Then read the fractions. $\frac{1}{3}$ $\frac{2}{5}$ $\frac{7}{10}$	explains how to use a fraction strip or a number line to show _____ $\frac{1}{3}$. _____ $\frac{2}{5}$. _____ $\frac{7}{10}$. correctly reads the fraction _____ $\frac{1}{3}$. _____ $\frac{2}{5}$. _____ $\frac{7}{10}$.
15-A.2 *To identify, read, and write mixed numbers and rename fractions greater than 1 as mixed numbers* Explain how you would name a fraction and a mixed number for the shaded parts.	_____ explains that the squares are divided into fourths and 15 parts are shaded, so $\frac{15}{4}$ is shaded. _____ explains that 3 whole squares and $\frac{3}{4}$ of the fourth square are shaded, so $3\frac{3}{4}$ is shaded.
15-A.3 *To compare fractions with unlike denominators* Explain how you would use the least common multiple to compare these fractions. $\frac{6}{8} \bigcirc \frac{5}{6}$	_____ explains that you first find the least common multiple (LCM) of the denominators. _____ names 24 as the LCM. _____ rewrites each fraction with a denominator of 24: $\frac{6}{8} = \frac{18}{24}$ and $\frac{5}{6} = \frac{20}{24}$. _____ identifies $\frac{20}{24} > \frac{18}{24}$ because 20 is greater than 18.
15-A.4 *To order fractions and draw a diagram to solve problems* Show and explain each step as you order these fractions from least to greatest. $\frac{1}{2}$ $\frac{3}{4}$ $\frac{2}{3}$	_____ explains how to write equivalent fractions with like denominators or locates the fractions on a number line. _____ identifies the order as $\frac{1}{2}, \frac{2}{3}, \frac{3}{4}$.

TEST ITEM	EVALUATE WHETHER STUDENT
16-A.1 *To find the greatest common factor of two numbers* Explain how you would find the greatest common factor of 18 and 24.	_____ explains that you first list the factors of each number; factors of 18: 1, 2, 3, 6, 9; factors of 24: 1, 2, 3, 4, 6, 8, 12. _____ identifies the common factors as 1, 2, 3, and 6. _____ identifies the greatest common factor as 6.
16-A.2 *To find equivalent fractions* Show and explain each step as you use fraction strips or number lines to determine which of these fractions are equivalent to $\frac{2}{3}$. $\frac{6}{9}$ $\frac{4}{8}$ $\frac{4}{6}$	_____ explains how to model the fractions on fraction strips or on a number line. _____ identifies $\frac{6}{9}$ and $\frac{4}{6}$ as fractions equivalent to $\frac{2}{3}$.
16-A.3 *To find the simplest form of a fraction* Explain how to use fraction bars to help you write $\frac{8}{12}$ in simplest form.	_____ explains that you line up fraction bars to find equivalent fractions for $\frac{8}{12}$ and look for the fraction that uses the largest fraction bar possible. _____ identifies $\frac{2}{3}$ as the simplest form for $\frac{8}{12}$.

Student's Name _____

Materials: fraction strips, fraction bars

TEST ITEM	EVALUATE WHETHER STUDENT
17-A.1 *To add fractions with like denominators* Show and explain each step as you use fraction strips to find the sum of $\frac{3}{8} + \frac{7}{8}$. Draw a picture to show what you did.	_____ aligns the bars or strips for $\frac{3}{8}$ and $\frac{7}{8}$ under 1-strips. _____ counts the total number of eighths strips and indicates there are 10 strips in all. _____ identifies the sum as $\frac{10}{8}$, or $1\frac{2}{8} = 1\frac{1}{4}$. _____ draws an appropriate picture for the model.
17-A.2 *To use least common denominator to add fractions with unlike denominators* Show and explain each step as you use fraction strips and the least common denominator to find the sum of $\frac{1}{2} + \frac{2}{5} + \frac{3}{10}$, and write the sum in simplest form. Draw a picture to show what you did.	_____ aligns the strips for the fractions for $\frac{1}{2}$, $\frac{2}{5}$, and $\frac{3}{10}$ under 1-strips. _____ indicates that 10 is the least common denominator of 2, 5, and 10. _____ uses like fraction strips for tenths to show the three fractions. _____ identifies the sum as $\frac{12}{10}$, or $1\frac{2}{10} = 1\frac{1}{5}$. _____ draws an appropriate picture for the model.

Student's Name _____

Materials: fraction strips, inch ruler

TEST ITEM	EVALUATE WHETHER STUDENT
18-A.1 *To subtract fractions with like denominators* Show and explain each step as you use fraction strips to find the difference of $\frac{7}{8} - \frac{3}{8}$. Draw a picture to show what you did.	_____ uses fraction strips to show either the take-away model or the comparison model. _____ identifies the difference as $\frac{4}{8}$, or $\frac{1}{2}$. _____ draws an appropriate picture for the model.
18-A.2 *To use least common denominator to subtract fractions with unlike denominators* Show and explain each step as you use fraction strips and the least common denominator to find the difference of $\frac{5}{6} - \frac{1}{4}$, and write the difference in simplest form. Draw a picture to show what you did.	_____ uses fraction strips to model the problem. _____ indicates that 12 is the least common denominator of 6 and 4. _____ uses like fraction strips for twelfths to show the difference. _____ identifies the difference as $\frac{7}{12}$. _____ draws an appropriate picture for the model.
18-A.3 *To subtract fractions of an inch on a ruler* Show and explain each step as you use a ruler to find the difference of $\frac{1}{2}$ in. $- \frac{1}{8}$ in. Draw a picture to show what you did.	_____ uses a ruler to model the problem. _____ identifies the difference as $\frac{3}{8}$ in. _____ draws an appropriate picture for the model.

Date _____

Student's Name _____

TEST ITEM	EVALUATE WHETHER STUDENT
19-A.1 *To estimate fractions and sums and differences of fractions* Estimate the sum or difference. Explain your methods. $\frac{1}{8} + \frac{5}{9}$ $\frac{9}{10} - \frac{7}{8}$	_____ explains that if the numerator is much less than the denominator, the fraction is close to 0. _____ explains that if the numerator is about one half the denominator, the fraction is close to $\frac{1}{2}$. _____ explains that if the numerator is about the same as the denominator, the fraction is close to 1. _____ identifies the estimated sum as about $0 + \frac{1}{2} = \frac{1}{2}$. _____ identifies the estimated difference as about $1 - 1 = 0$.
19-A.2 *To add and subtract like and unlike fractions* Show and explain each step as you find the sum or difference. Write the answers in simplest form. $\frac{5}{6} + \frac{3}{6}$ $\frac{3}{5} - \frac{1}{2}$	for the first problem: _____ explains that because the denominators are the same, you can add the numerators and put the sum over the denominator: $\frac{8}{6}$. _____ writes the sum in simplest form: $\frac{8}{6} = 1\frac{2}{6} = 1\frac{1}{3}$. for the second problem: _____ explains that because the denominators are different, you must first change the fractions to like fractions: $\frac{3}{5} = \frac{6}{10}$ and $\frac{1}{2} = \frac{5}{10}$. _____ subtracts the numerators and puts the difference over the denominator: $\frac{1}{10}$. _____ explains that the difference is in simplest form.
19-A.3 *To solve problems by choosing the operation and drawing a diagram* Explain each step as you draw a diagram to solve this problem. *Mr. Erickson asked the students in his class whether they prefer to have a pizza party, a bagel party, or a taco party. Of the students, $\frac{1}{8}$ chose pizza, $\frac{3}{8}$ chose bagel, and $\frac{1}{2}$ chose taco. There were 4 students who chose pizza. How many students are in Mr. Erickson's class?*	_____ draws an appropriate diagram for the problem. _____ identifies the number of students who chose a bagel party as 12 and the number of students who chose a taco party as 16. _____ identifies the total number of students in Mr. Erickson's class as 32.

TEST ITEM	EVALUATE WHETHER STUDENT
20-A.1 *To estimate sums and differences of mixed numbers* Estimate the sum or difference. Explain your methods. $2\frac{1}{5} + 1\frac{5}{6}$ $5\frac{9}{10} - 2\frac{4}{9}$	_____ explains that you can estimate sums and differences by first estimating each fraction to the nearest whole number or one half. _____ identifies the estimated sum as about $2 + 2 = 4$. _____ identifies the estimated difference as about $6 - 2\frac{1}{2} = 3\frac{1}{2}$.
20-A.2 *To add mixed numbers* Show and explain each step as you find the sum. Write the answer in simplest form. $2\frac{3}{4} + 4\frac{1}{2}$	_____ estimates the sum as about $7\frac{1}{2}$. _____ explains that because the fractions are unlike, you must first use the lowest common denominator (LCD) to change the fractions to like fractions. _____ adds the fractions: $\frac{3}{4} + \frac{2}{4} = \frac{5}{4}$, or $1\frac{1}{4}$ _____ adds the whole numbers: $2 + 4 = 6$. _____ adds the partial sums: $6 + 1\frac{1}{4} = 7\frac{1}{4}$. _____ identifies the sum in simplest form as $7\frac{1}{4}$.
To subtract mixed numbers Show and explain each step as you find the difference. Write the answer in simplest form. $3\frac{2}{3} - 1\frac{1}{2}$	_____ estimates the difference as about $2\frac{1}{2}$ (or 2). _____ explains that because the fractions are unlike, you must first use the LCD to change the fractions to like fractions. _____ subtracts the fractions: $\frac{4}{6} - \frac{3}{6} = \frac{1}{6}$. _____ subtracts the whole numbers: $3 - 1 = 2$. _____ combines the partial differences. _____ identifies the difference in simplest form as $2\frac{1}{6}$.

Evaluation of Interview/Task Test

Date _____

CHAPTER 21

Student's Name _____

Materials: analog clock, Fahrenheit thermometer (optional)

TEST ITEM	EVALUATE WHETHER STUDENT
21-A.1 *To compute and change units of measurement by multiplying or dividing* Explain how you know whether to multiply or divide when changing from one customary unit to another. Explain how you know how to complete these statements. 18 ft = _?_ yd 3 pt = _?_ c 48 oz = _?_ lb Then show and explain each step as you find the sum. 6 ft 8 in. + 2 ft 9 in. _____	_____ explains that you multiply to change units to smaller units and divide to change units to larger units. _____ 18 ft = 6 yards; divide by 3 because there are 3 feet in a yard. _____ 3 pt = 6 c; multiply by 2 because there are 2 cups in a pint. _____ 48 oz = 3 lb; divide by 16 because there are 16 ounces in a pound. _____ explains that to find the sum you add each kind of unit and then rename and combine units, if you need to. _____ identifies the sum as 9 ft 5 in.
21-A.2 *To find elapsed time* Determine the elapsed time from 10:30 A.M. to 2:45 P.M.. Explain your method.	_____ chooses an appropriate method to determine elapsed time, such as *counting forward* on a clock from the starting time to the ending time. _____ identifies the elapsed time as 4 hr 15 min.
21-A.3 *To read Fahrenheit and Celsius thermometers and compare differences in temperature* Explain how you would find the difference between an outside temperature of 55°F and an indoor temperature of 78°F.	_____ explains that you would subtract to find the difference in temperature. _____ identifies the difference as 23°F.

Student's Name _____

Materials: fraction square

TEST ITEM	EVALUATE WHETHER STUDENT
22-A.1 *To multiply a fraction by a whole number* Draw a picture or multiply to find the product. Explain the method you use. Write the product in simplest form. $$\frac{1}{3} \times 12 = n$$	_____ explains how to draw a picture or multiply to find the product. _____ identifies the product in simplest form as 4.
22-A.2 *To multiply two fractions* Use a fraction square or multiply to find the product. Explain the method you use. Write the answer in simplest form. $$\frac{5}{6} \times \frac{2}{3} = n$$	_____ explains how to use a fraction square or multiply to find the product. _____ identifies the product in simplest form as $\frac{5}{9}$.
22-A.3 *To multiply a fraction by a mixed number* Use fraction squares or multiply to find the product. Explain the method you use. Write the answer in simplest form. $$\frac{1}{3} \times 3\frac{1}{4} = n$$	_____ explains how to use a fraction square or multiply to find the product. _____ identifies the product in simplest form as $1\frac{1}{12}$.

Evaluation of Interview/Task Test

Date _____

Student's Name_____

Materials: grid paper

TEST ITEM	EVALUATE WHETHER STUDENT
23-A.1 *To identify line relationships, rays, and angles* Explain your choices as you name classroom objects that remind you of intersecting lines, perpendicular lines, parallel lines, a ray, a right angle, an acute angle, and an obtuse angle.	selects appropriate classroom objects and states characteristics of the objects to explain why they were chosen for: _____ intersecting lines. _____ perpendicular lines. _____ parallel lines. _____ a ray. _____ a right angle. _____ an acute angle. _____ an obtuse angle.
23-A.2 *To solve problems by using a diagram* Use grid paper to make a map for the directions given for getting from the house to Spring Lake. First, mark the top of the paper as north, the bottom as south, the left as west, and the right as east. Draw a house at the intersection of two lines near the top left corner of the paper. *From the house, go 4 blocks east. Make a 90° turn south onto Main Street. Drive 6 blocks south, and make a 90 °turn east onto Second Avenue. Drive 5 blocks and make a 90° turn south onto Lake Street. Drive 3 blocks to Spring Lake.*	_____ labels the grid paper correctly. _____ draws an appropriate map for the directions.
23-A.3 *To classify quadrilaterals and triangles* Draw a trapezoid, a parallelogram, a rectangle, a square, an isosceles triangle, and an equilateral triangle. Next to each figure, write a description of the figure.	correctly draws and describes: _____ a trapezoid. _____ a parallelogram. _____ a rectangle. _____ a square. _____ an isosceles triangle. _____ an equilateral triangle.

Materials: grid paper

TEST ITEM	EVALUATE WHETHER STUDENT
24-A.1 *To identify congruent figures* On grid paper, draw two figures that are congruent. Describe two methods you could use to test for congruency.	_____ draws two congruent figures. _____ explains that you can test for congruency by putting the two figures on top of each other to see if they match. _____ explains that you can test for congruency by measuring the length of each side and the size of each angle of the figures.
24-A.2 *To identify multiple lines of symmetry in a figure or an object* Use a square piece of paper. Fold the paper to show as many lines of symmetry as you can. Draw a diagram to show the lines of symmetry you found.	_____ folds the square to show lines of symmetry. _____ explains that there are 4 lines of symmetry. _____ draws a diagram to show the lines of symmetry.
24-A.3 *To transform a figure on a coordinate grid* Draw a triangle on grid paper and label it *original figure.* Then draw new triangles to show a *translation,* a *reflection,* and a *rotation.* Label the new triangles. Explain how you moved the original triangle to show each new triangle.	_____ draws the original triangle on grid paper. _____ draws a translation and explains that a translation slides the triangle in one direction. _____ draws a reflection and explains that a reflection flips the figure over a line. _____ draws a rotation and explained that a rotation turns the figure.
24-A.4 *To transform a figure to make a tessellation* Explain what a tessellation is. Then copy this figure and translate, reflect, or rotate it to make a design that tessellates.	_____ explains that a tessellation is an arrangement of figures that covers a surface with no gaps and no overlaps. _____ copies the figure correctly and makes a design that tessellates.

Evaluation of Interview/Task Test

Date_____

CHAPTER 25

Student's Name_____

Materials: string, ruler, round counter, compass, protractor

TEST ITEM	EVALUATE WHETHER STUDENT
25-A.1 *To identify parts of a circle such as a chord, a diameter, and a radius* Construct a circle. Draw and label a chord, a diameter, and a radius. Describe these parts of a circle.	_____ constructs a circle. draws and labels: _____ a chord. _____ a diameter. _____ a radius. describes: _____ a chord. _____ a diameter. _____ a radius.
25-A.2 *To investigate finding the circumference of a circle* Show and explain each step as you use string and a ruler to measure the circumference and the diameter of a round counter. Then explain how the diameter and the circumference are related.	_____ wraps string around the counter and measures the length of the string with a ruler. _____ measures the diameter of the counter. _____ explains that the circumference is about 3 times greater than the diameter, or $C \div d$ is 3.14.
25-A.3 *To identify angle measures in a circle and find missing angle measures* Draw a pie sliced in half. Then slice one of the halves in half. Explain how to find the number of degrees in the angles of the sliced pie.	_____ explains that the whole pie has 360°. _____ explains that the first slice forms two 180° angles. _____ explains that the second slice divides one of the 180° angles into two 90° angles.
25-A.4 *To divide a circle according to given angle measures* Show and explain each step as you use a compass and a protractor to draw a circle with 2 angles of 60° each and two angles of 120° each.	_____ draws a circle with a compass. _____ uses a protractor correctly to draw the 4 angles.

TEST ITEM	EVALUATE WHETHER STUDENT
26-A.1 *To name and classify prisms and pyramids* Explain how prisms and pyramids are named. Tell how they are different and how they are the same. Then name a classroom object that reminds you of a prism and a classroom object that reminds you of a pyramid.	_____ explains how a prism and a pyramid are different. _____ explains how a prism and a pyramid are alike. _____ names a classroom object for a prism and a pyramid.
26-A.2 *To identify a two-dimensional pattern for a three-dimensional solid* Look at the three nets on page 457, Exercise 9. Name the three-dimensional figure that could be formed from each of the three nets. Explain how you know which figure can be formed.	_____ explains that *net a* forms a triangular pyramid because its base is a triangle and its faces are triangles. _____ explains that *net b* forms a square pyramid because its base is a square and its faces are triangles. _____ explains that *net c* forms a triangular prism because its two bases are triangles and its faces are rectangles.
26-A.3 *To use a formula to solve a problem* Explain each step as you use a formula to solve this problem. Scott has a carton that is 25 cm long and 20 cm wide. The carton has a volume of 5,000 cubic centimeters. Can Scott fit a box that is 20 cm long, 15 cm wide, and 12 cm high in the carton?	_____ uses the formula $V = l \times w \times h$ to find the missing dimension of the carton. _____ identifies the missing dimension as 10 cm. _____ states that the box will not fit because the box is 12 cm high and the carton is only 10 cm high.
26-A.4 *To estimate the volume of a rectangular prism in cubic units* Use a 1-cm cube as a benchmark to estimate the volume of a small paper-clip box. Explain your method.	_____ explains that you can use the cube as a benchmark to estimate the length, width, and height of the box and then use the formula for volume to estimate the volume of the box. _____ gives a reasonable estimate for the length (about 7 cm), the width (about 5 cm), the height (about 2 cm) and the volume (about 70 cubic cm) of the box.

Evaluation of Interview/Task Test

Date _____

CHAPTER 27

Student's Name _____

Materials: two-color counters, map on PE page 482, centimeter ruler, Exercise 4 on PE page 485

TEST ITEM	EVALUATE WHETHER STUDENT
27-A.1 *To express ratios in three ways* Toss a handful of two-color counters. Write the ratio of red counters to yellow counters in three different ways. Explain and write other ratios for the counters.	_____ writes the ratio of red to yellow in three different ways (r to y, $r:y$, $\frac{r}{y}$). _____ explains and writes other ratios for the counters. (Possible ratios: yellow to red, red to all, all to red, yellow to all, all to yellow)
27-A.2 *To identify and make equivalent ratios* Toss 8 two-color counters. Write the ratio of red counters to yellow counters. Then write 3 ratios that are equivalent to that ratio. Explain how the 4 ratios are related.	_____ writes a ratio for red counters to yellow counters. _____ writes three equivalent ratios. _____ explains that the ratios all show the same relationship.
27-A.3 *To use ratios to interpret map scales* Look at the map of Texas on page 482. Measure the distance from El Paso to Houston in centimeters. Then explain how to use the map distance and the map scale to find the actual distance from El Paso to Houston.	_____ measures the map distance from El Paso to Houston in centimeters. _____ uses the map distance and the map scale to determine the actual distance from El Paso to Houston. _____ explains that to find the actual distance, you multiply both numbers in the ratio for the map scale by the map distance.
27-A.4 *To use equivalent ratios to determine the sides of similar figures* Look at the similar triangles in Exercise 7 on page 485. The length of the longest side in the larger triangle is 30 units. Explain how you would find the length of the longest side of the smaller triangle.	_____ explains that in similar figures, matching sides have equivalent ratios. _____ writes equivalent ratios, such as $\frac{18 \div 2}{30 \div 2} = \frac{9}{15}$, to find the missing length. _____ identifies the missing length as 15 units.

Performance Assessme

TEST ITEM	EVALUATE WHETHER STUDENT
28-A.1 *To write a percent as a decimal* In a hundreds decimal square, shade some of the squares red, shade some blue, and shade the rest yellow. Explain how you know how to write both a decimal and a percent for the part of the square that is red, the part that is blue, and the part that is yellow.	_____ explains that a percent compares a part to 100 and a decimal represents a number of hundredths. _____ identifies the correct percent for red, blue, and yellow. _____ identifies the correct decimal for red, blue, and yellow.
28-A.2 *To write a percent as a fraction* Look at the hundreds square you colored in the task above. Explain how you know how to write a fraction for the percent of the square that is red, the part that is blue, and the part that is yellow.	_____ explains that since a percent compares a part to 100, you can represent the number as a fraction—the part as the numerator and 100 as the denominator. _____ identifies the correct fraction for red, blue, and yellow.
28-A.3 *To use benchmarks to estimate percents* Use the hundreds square you colored in the task above. Which of the following benchmarks would you use to estimate the percent of the square that is red, the percent that is blue, and the percent that is yellow. Explain your choices. 10% 25% 50% 75% 100%	_____ identifies reasonable estimates for the percent of the hundreds square that is red, blue, and yellow. _____ explains why the percents are reasonable—for example, 25% is a good benchmark for amounts close to one fourth, and 50% is a good benchmark for amounts close to one half.
28-A.4 *To read percents from circle graphs* Use a circle divided into ten equal parts to make a circle graph to show the favorite school lunch of the fifth-grade students. Favorite Lunch Pizza 30% Hamburgers 10% Salad Bar 50% Tacos 10% Then explain how you can tell from looking at the graph which lunch one half of the students liked best.	_____ makes a correct circle graph for the data. _____ explains that you can tell that one half of the students liked the Salad Bar best because the section for Salad Bar is one half of the circle.

Performance Assessment

Class Record Form • Page 1

Teacher _____

1-A.1	To identify a number as ordinal, nominal, or cardinal														
1-A.2	To use benchmark numbers to estimate quantity														
1-A.3	To identify place value and read and identify numbers to millions														
1-A.4	To compare and order numbers to millions														
2-A.1	To use addition and subtraction as inverse operations														
2-A.2	To subtract across zeros with regrouping														
2-A.3	To choose the operation to solve problems														
2-A.4	To estimate sums and differences														
3-A.1	To read and write decimals in tenths and hundredths														
3-A.2	To read and write numbers from thousands to thousandths in standard and expanded form														
3-A.3	To identify and write equivalent decimals														
3-A.4	To compare and order decimals														

Performance Assessment

Class Record Form • Page 2

Teacher _____

4-A.1	To add and subtract decimals																	
4-A.2	To estimate decimals, sums and differences																	
4-A.3	To solve problems by choosing the operation and writing a number sentence																	
5-A.1	To identify and use multiplication properties																	
5-A.2	To multiply by one-digit numbers																	
5-A.3	To use formulas to find area and volume																	
6-A.1	To multiply by two- or three-digit numbers																	
6-A.2	To estimate products																	
6-A.3	To multiply to find perimeter and area																	
7-A.1	To estimate a quotient																	
7-A.2	To divide by one-digit numbers																	
7-A.3	To solve problems by using the *guess-and-check* strategy																	

Performance Assessment

MATH ADVANTAGE
Grade 5

Class Record Form • Page 3

Teacher _____

8-A.1	To use patterns of zeros and estimation to divide																												
8-A.2	To estimate quotients																												
8-A.3	To divide by two-digit numbers																												
8-A.4	To solve problems by choosing the operation and writing a number sentence																												
9-A.1	To compute the mean of a set of data																												
9-A.2	To choose a reasonable scale for a set of data																												
9-A.3	To make and use line graphs																												
9-A.4	To choose the appropriate graph to display data																												
10-A.1	To read and interpret circle graphs																												
10-A.2	To determine whether data are accurate and choose the best type of graph to display data																												
10-A.3	To compare data displayed in different kinds of graphs																												

Performance Assessment

Class Record Form • Page 4

Teacher _____

11-A.1	To determine whether events are certain, impossible, or likely																								
11-A.2	To make a tree diagram and solve problems by making a list																								
11-A.3	To find the probability of an event and compare probabilities of separate events																								
12-A.1	To identify and use patterns in decimal factors and products																								
12-A.2	To multiply decimals by whole numbers and decimals by decimals																								
12-A.3	To use estimation to place the decimal point in the product																								
12-A.4	To multiply mixed decimals																								
13-A.1	To identify patterns when dividing multiples of ten																								
13-A.2	To divide decimals by whole numbers and use patterns or estimation to place the decimal																								
13-A.3	To choose the operation to solve problems																								

MATH ADVANTAGE
Grade 5

Performance Assessment

Class Record Form • Page 5

Teacher _____

14-A.1	To measure length in metric units																						
14-A.2	To use metric units to measure the mass of objects																						
14-A.3	To identify the relationship between metric units																						
15-A.1	To identify, read, and write fractions																						
15-A.2	To identify, read, and write mixed numbers and to rename fractions greater than 1 as mixed numbers																						
15-A.3	To compare fractions with unlike denominators																						
15-A.4	To order fractions and draw a diagram to solve problems																						
16-A.1	To find the greatest common factor of two numbers																						
16-A.2	To find equivalent fractions																						
16-A.3	To find the simplest form of a fraction																						
17-A.1	To add fractions with like denominators																						
17-A.2	To use the least common denominator to add fractions with unlike denominators																						

108

Performance Assessment

Class Record Form • Page 6

Teacher _____

18-A.1	To subtract fractions with like denominators																			
18-A.2	To use the least common denominator to subtract fractions with unlike denominators																			
18-A.3	To subtract fractions of an inch on a ruler																			
19-A.1	To estimate fractions and sums and differences of fractions																			
19-A.2	To add and subtract like and unlike fractions																			
19-A.3	To solve problems by choosing the operation and drawing a diagram																			
20-A.1	To estimate sums and differences of mixed numbers																			
20-A.2	To add and subtract mixed numbers																			
21-A.1	To compute and change units of measurement by multiplying or dividing																			
21-A.2	To determine amount of elapsed time																			
21-A.3	To read Fahrenheit and Celsius thermometers and to compare difference in two temperatures																			

Performance Assessment

Class Record Form • Page 7

Teacher _____

22-A.1	To multiply a fraction by a whole number
22-A.2	To multiply two fractions
22-A.3	To multiply a fraction by a mixed number
23-A.1	To identify line relationships, rays, and angles
23-A.2	To solve problems by using a diagram
23-A.3	To classify quadrilaterals and triangles
24-A.1	To identify congruent figures
24-A.2	To identify multiple lines of symmetry in a figure or an object
24-A.3	To transform a figure on a coordinate grid
24-A.4	To transform a figure to make a tessellation
25-A.1	To identify parts of a circle, such as chord, diameter, and radius
25-A.2	To investigate finding the circumference of a circle
25-A.3	To identify angle measures in a circle and find missing angle measures
25-A.4	To divide a circle according to given angle measures

Performance Assessment

Class Record Form • Page 8

Teacher _____

26-A.1	To name and classify prisms and pyramids																		
26-A.2	To identify a two-dimensional pattern for a three-dimensional solid																		
26-A.3	To use a formula to solve a problem																		
26-A.4	To estimate the volume of a rectangular prism in cubic units																		
27-A.1	To express ratios in three ways																		
27-A.2	To identify and make equivalent ratios																		
27-A.3	To use ratios to interpret map scales																		
27-A.4	To use equivalent ratios to determine the sides of similar figures																		
28-A.1	To write a percent as a decimal																		
28-A.2	To write a percent as a fraction																		
28-A.3	To use benchmarks to estimate percents																		
28-A.4	To read percents from circle graphs																		